Empowering Authority

The Charisms of Episcopacy and Primacy in the Church Today

Papers delivered at Annual Symposia,
1987-1988-1989
Seattle University

edited by
Gary Chamberlain
Patrick J. Howell, S.J.

Sheed & Ward

Sheed & Ward™ is a service of National Catholic Reporter Publishing
Company, Inc.

Library of Congress Catalog Card Number: 90-60902

ISBN: 1-55612-360-4

Published by: Sheed & Ward
                 115 E. Armour Blvd. P.O. Box 419492
                 Kansas City, MO 64141

To order, call: (800) 333-7373

Contents

Preface: Re-Imaging Authority in the Church
  Dr. Gary Chamberlain and Fr. Pat Howell v

1. Catholicism and Living Tradition:
   The Church as a Community of Reception, *Fr. Michael Scanlon* . 1

2. Authority, Women, and Church:
   Reconsidering the Relationship, *Sr. Anne Patrick* 17

3. Freedom, Responsibility, Authority, *Fr. David Tracy* 34

4. The Doctrinal Limits
   to Papal Teaching Authority, *Fr. Peter Chirico* 48

5. Feminist Analysis and Church Authority:
   Reflections on Recent North American
   Episcopal Statements on Women, *Sr. Mary Ellen Sheehan* . . . 65

6. Two Views of the Church:
   The United States and the Vatican, *Fr. Richard McBrien* . . . 81

7. Authority in the Twentieth Century:
   "Whose Image and Whose Inscription?"
   A Biblical Reflection, *Dr. Karen Barta* 103

8. Issues Orbiting Church Authority, *Fr. Michael Raschko* . . . 116

Contributors to this Volume 128

Vatican Investigation: Chronology of Events 130

Introduction

Re-Imaging Authority in the Church

A Brief Background

After an official visitation of the Seattle Catholic Church by Archbishop James Hickey, the Vatican critiqued the ministry of Archbishop Raymond Hunthausen in December, 1985, and sent a newly appointed bishop, Donald Wuerl of the Pittsburgh Diocese, to remedy the "errors." Following this Vatican intervention theologians, parishes, lay leaders, and priests gathered spontaneously to reflect and to pray over the implicit accusation of unfaithfulness against the local church. This intervention through delegates reporting to Pope John Paul II, then in his seventh year as Bishop of Rome, precipitated a faith crisis in some, a vigorous protest by many, a satisfied "at last!" by a few.

During the 20 years following Vatican II, the mainstream Catholics in Seattle had responded with joy, with some sadness, with freedom, with occasional resistance to the challenge of the Council to embrace a new vision of the Church. Because of their location on the Pacific Rim they had a vantage of openness toward all peoples of faith. They welcomed the breaking open of Scriptures, they struggled with a preferential option for the poor. Locally, the "Church in the Modern World" was taking root and beginning to flourish. The ecumenical outreach of Seattle's Archbishop Raymond Hunthausen was well known. His pastoral leadership had encouraged many to involve themselves in the peace movement for a safer world and to confront the regional military installations and local armaments merchants.

These two currents of a more radical dedication to peace and of a steady renewal of the local Church triggered an unprecedented torrent of letters to Rome by some people who hoped for a restoration of Church to the period "before all the confusion started" and who felt their "American" values were deeply threatened by world communism and by "socialist" theology. At the very time that Archbishop Hunthausen was calling the Trident Missile Base at Bangor "The Auschwitz of the Puget Sound," the secular spokesman for these troubled Catholics, President Ronald Reagan, was denouncing the USSR as "the evil empire."

Some congregations in the Vatican, especially the Congregation for the Doctrine of the Faith headed by Cardinal Joseph Ratzinger, were also concerned about the American Church and its bishops. The Americans seemed to be "going too far." The "Vatican," by no means a monolithic group, needed to respond. Reportedly they singled out two bishops, the Bishop of Richmond, Virginia, and the Archbishop of Seattle for a visitation and for a critique of their ministry. The Vatican made its arrangements through the traditional post of the Papal Nuncio Pio Laghi, just recently elevated from the rank of papal delegate after a series of negotiations with the Reagan government. Just that year the Vatican had finally achieved full ambassadorial status by the American government, a struggle that had been continuous, even prior to the dissolution of the Papal States in 1873 when the popes still had territorial sovereignty through the mid-section of Italy.

Archbishop Laghi arranged for Archbishop James Hickey, the resident archbishop of Washington, DC, who resided just a few miles away, to conduct a visitation of Seattle. Later Archbishop Laghi was the conduit for Cardinal Ratzinger's secretly held criticisms about Hunthausen's ministry regarding the marriage tribunal, intercommunion, homosexual men and women, use of general absolution, sequence of first confession and first Communion, the role of women and other matters.

Laghi was a well-schooled diplomat. He had held the same post of papal nuncio in Argentina during the military regime's systemic extermination and torture of vocal oppression. In Washington, DC, Archbishop Laghi preferred to work behind the scenes and regularly turned down requests for interviews from journalists. Close to the centers of secular power, the nunciatura where he lived was a lovely mansion along embassy row on Massachusetts Avenue, not far from the British Embassy and across the street from the residence of Vice President George Bush.

Laghi's primary concern, however, centered on maintaining the traditional support of the American bishops for the Vatican. His talents for smooth, dependable diplomacy were well known; his pastoral experience was remote. Since 1980 when he assumed office from Archbishop Jean Jadot, Laghi had quietly and systematically installed bishops in American Sees who were supportive or at least neutral on the issues vital to the Vatican's agenda: a papal ban on discussing the possibility of women's ordination, support for "Humanae Vitae," and a ban on a married clergy. Laghi's predecessor, Archbishop Jadot, on the other hand, had made it his priority to select pastoral bishops of intelligence and sensitivity to the local church.

The stage was set for a major confrontation between two models of Church: a hierarchical, institutional model with concern for unity, on the one hand, and a prophetic, communal model with a pastoral concern for its people, on the other. These models were not exclusive. In fact, Avery Dulles recently described the two underlying theologies in this way: "In the council documents the theme of the Church as an organized society or institution is clearly subordinated to those of the Church as mystery, sacrament, and communion of grace. Yet the image of the People of God, which holds a major position in the Constitution on the Church, is developed in such as way as to imply institutional and hierarchical structures. The hierarchy, without detriment to its authority, is viewed as a service to the whole People of God."

These tensions embedded in the Council had grown through the years. What was urgent now was for respectful dialogue, universal teaching with integral, local differences, and a mutual learning by all. Some painful first steps have been made toward such a dialogue. In fact the symposia at Seattle University resulted in a better understanding of the *tradition* as a source of institutional and communal transformation.

After the long, tendentious investigation was concluded in April, 1989, Archbishop Hunthausen said: "Both Archbishop Murphy (the new coadjutor of Seattle) and I acknowledge the trial the church here has faced over the past several years, yet we are also able to view the whole experience as a time of grace, a grace which, with the Lord's help, will enable us to offer our leadership in Western Washington in the years ahead with renewed dedication and commitment to the gospel and the universal church under our Holy Father, Pope John Paul II.

"We ask for your prayers as we continue to meet the challenges of being a Roman Catholic Community of faith here in Western Washington," Hunthausen concluded.

During a somewhat more tranquil time, the Theology Department of Seattle University and the Catholic Theological Society of America (CTSA) co-sponsored a Symposium on "Episcopacy and Primacy" in December, 1987. Two other symposia in 1988 and 1989 continued the discussion between nationally noted theologians and local pastoral leaders.

Context of the Symposium

Over 25 years ago theologians Karl Rahner and Joseph Ratzinger published their major work, *The Episcopacy and Primacy*. The positions which Rahner and Ratzinger outlined in 1962 represent two views which clash resoundingly in the struggles over authority in the church. Rahner said, "When a bishop by taking some initiative . . . does something destined to enrich the whole Church, then this is not presumption or exceeding his competence, but a part of exercising his office and his duty." Ratzinger, however, emphasized the hierarchical view dominant since Vatican I: "First, it is the certain teaching of the church that the pope has immediate, ordinary, truly episcopal power of jurisdiction over the whole Church." Rahner's view suggests that supporting the local church and by extension building regional and national coordination among bishops enhance the mission of the Church in the modern world. At the same time a more decentralized church serves peoples' immediate needs and supports their living faith with a sensitivity to the local context and a respect for the independence of adult peoples.

Issues of power and authority and of relationships between local churches and Rome ultimately intertwine with the fundamental questions of the church's mission and meaning in the modern world. Given the variety of cultural contexts in which the church finds itself today a uniform set of policies, procedures, and practices passed down from a centralized authority does not fit the varied expressions of Christian faith in the world. The Second Vatican Council's "Pastoral Constitution on the Church" recognized the issue, but only now are we experiencing and understanding the full implications of a true "mission to the world." We are caught in the torturous movement toward a world church.

Such a mission must respect the authentic spirit of differing peoples all over the world while translating the central truths of the Catholic, Christian faith into forms and expressions which are understood and appropriated by local peoples. This cultural differentiation is often as true within a nation as between nations. For example, the church in the Pacific Northwest, so small in numbers, resting upon the labors of recent immigrants and without a long ecclesiastical tradition requires a flexible, open style of governance and pastoral practice. The churches in urban New York city or rural Minnesota demand their own adaptations. And the church in the United States necessitates a mode of theological understanding and pastoral activity much different from that needed in churches in Latin America, Asia or Italy.

In the midst of these rich varieties of expression, how does the center hold? Amid the babble of voices, what authority speaks "authentically"? How is "authority" authentically expressed so that it is received as authentic by the local people of God? The slow and agonizing movement toward a truly world church challenges past certitudes about the roles of pope, bishop, and people of God. Other basic questions about human life issues, peace and justice questions, the roles of women in church and society, and the place of laypeople in church structure and ministry are all subsumed under the overriding question of power and authority. Fulsome clashes on church teaching and practices more often reflect radically different conceptions and interpretations of authority.

With a tradition of collegiality among bishops and the increasing role of lay people, the church in the United States is articulating a sense of mission for an educated, urbanized society characterized by an excessive individualism and by a tradition of resistance to authority. Thus the church in the Unites States has its own complex issues to address as well as its own contribution to make for the universal church.

The dialogues in this volume represent an attempt by a local church, the Archdiocese of Seattle, to examine an issue critical to its existence. During the Vatican investigation the local church challenged the method and purpose of the Vatican's inquiry. At the heart of its struggles with the Vatican were not only questions of the church's teaching on liturgy, sexuality, and doctrinal unity but more importantly the authenticity to the Gospel of the local church as "People of God."

In living out the challenges and call to renewal of Vatican II the Archdiocese of Seattle has developed a mode of lay involvement and episcopal leadership which provides a model for other local churches. The investigation, although framed around narrow issues, reflected an altogether different model of church, as Richard McBrien and Peter Chirico articulate in this volume, in which authority is necessarily hierarchical and dialogue is turned into monologue. The chill emanating from the investigation still hovers over the Archdiocese of Western Washington even after the investigation concluded with full restoration of his powers to Archbishop Hunthausen. How the "people of God" model of church will fare in the future is unclear. The reflections presented in this volume unravel the perplexing questions of the identity, authority, and meaning of a pilgrim church seeking to walk in the footsteps of Jesus, the Christ. In particular, they lay the ground for further development of a dialogical and vital relationship between local church and universal church in which authority emerges in the church by virtue of the authenticity of the office bearer.

The Participants

The volume contains the eight major talks of the symposia. The conferences were marked by tranquil reflection, theological exploration, and pastoral concern. The exchanges were respectful, often spiritual, and we hope will invite a continuing conversation.

Fr. Michael Scanlon, O.S.A., the 1988 President of CTSA, opened the 1987 proceedings. His paper makes a bold argument for radical change using a deconstructing treatment of tradition and retrieving the role of authentic authority as being one of serving the Church in a process of discernment of the "sensus fidelium," that is, the lived faith of the faithful. After exploring Hans Gadamer's distinction between "authority" and "authoritarianism," Scanlon urges a renewal of the ancient hermeneutic in which dialogue and discernment are a communal enterprise.

Sr. Anne Patrick, S.N.J.M., the 1989 President of CTSA, considers the issue of authority from an ethical perspective and within the context of a growing conviction of the fundamental equality of women and men and that God's Spirit is given to all the faithful, not only to those in positions of hierarchical office. Adapting categories of H. Richard Niebuhr, she maps out a spectrum of five responses of women to ecclesial oppression and opts primarily for the fifth, that of "women transforming the church."

Fr. David Tracy, University of Chicago, situates theology in its academic context and argues that the proposals theologians make for theology *as theology* must be judged by criteria in the academy. The academy is the only relevant authority, Tracy explains, of professional competence and scholarship. The responsibility of the theologian in the academy is never to allow oneself to express unexamined private opinion as public proposals.

When theologians address proposals to the church or society, Tracy says, they must also take into account *de jure* and *de facto* authorities of that particular society. American bishops, for instance, make their arguments in their pastorals on inner-Christian and inner-Catholic grounds *and* they try to make an argument for the wider society on grounds it can accept. Likewise, the theologian, grounded and critiqued by colleagues in the academy, makes proposals for the People of God for their discernment for responding to God's call. The *de facto* authorities' role is to assist in this discernment; their role is not to determine theological competency. That is the responsibility of the academy.

In the second symposium a year later, in 1988, three other theologians continued to explore the issues relating to authority in the church.

In his paper *Fr. Peter Chirico, S.S.,* at that time dean of St. Patrick's Seminary, Menlo Park, California, and currently a faculty member of the Institute for Theological Studies, Seattle University, says that practically nothing in the Church's official teaching deals extensively with the obligations of the papacy and the limits of its powers. In a careful exploration, Fr. Chirico examines the doctrinal limits to papal teaching authority. These limits flow very naturally from the nature of the papal office and are binding. One clear example is that only universal objective faith meanings can be the object of definition by the pope's infallible magisterium. The bishops, Chirico says, do a disservice to the Church if they rubber stamp papal teaching because the pope may not have fulfilled the conditions of such teaching. The function of all Church teaching is to illumine and to clarify what is already faith experience.

Sr. Mary Ellen Sheehan, I.H.M., St. Michael's College, University of Toronto, traces the progressive development toward feminist analysis in the pastorals of some North American bishops and concludes that the global transformation of consciousness regarding women has just begun. Though some bishops have made notable strides, the episcopacy is hardly yet at the starting gate, she concludes.

Fr. Richard McBrien, University of Notre Dame, compares the ecclesiology of most U.S. Catholic theologians and pastoral ministers with the ecclesiology of the principal centers of power in the Vatican. He examines the foundational differences of these two views within the sessions of Vatican II and in the political maneuvering which has followed. Finally, he gives extensive examples drawn from American political life to illustrate how a political dynamic affects communal interaction, whether secular or ecclesial.

In the third symposium, held in 1989, two theologians from Seattle continued the scrutiny of issues of authority within the church.

Dr. Karen Barta takes up the challenge of authority by examining paternalism and autonomy as the two major forms of authority experienced in the post-industrial world. Beginning with Richard Sennett's analysis of authority and leadership styles, she transfers those images underlying the dominant modes of authority in modern society to an analysis of authority in the Church. In the second part of the paper, Dr. Barta carefully and concisely offers a biblical response to these images of authority, suggesting how biblical stories and metaphors can liberate our imaginations from the corrosive images of paternalism. Through such a process of re-imaging, the practice of authority within the Church can become a means for mutual empowerment.

Fr. Michael B. Raschko looks at four issues which shape how ecclesial authority is viewed and exercised. The first issue is the theological notion of *jus divinum,* which claims a divine mandate and permanence for certain structures and objects of Church authority. The second is "the analogical circle," which explores how images of God are rooted in human experience, but then take on a life of their own and give to human structures a divine authority. The third issue is sexuality, which is often not only the object of the exercise of ecclesial authority, but also a powerful hidden factor in how authority functions in the Church. The fourth issue is hermeneutics. In a Church which is active in many contemporary cultures and spans many different epochs in the history of the West, the exercise of ecclesial authority, informed by explicitly hermeneutical principles, is essential.

We are especially grateful for all those who made this project possible and for the support of the Theology and Religious Studies Department and the Institute for Theological Studies, both of Seattle University, the Lay Ministries Department of the Seattle Archdiocese, and the Roy Street Jesuit Community. We were deeply appreciative of the Catholic Theological Society of America and its 1987-1988 President, Michael Scanlon, O.S.A., who willingly agreed to co-sponsor the first symposium.

We were immeasurably assisted in these preparations by Lisa Ursino, and, most of all, by Gary Dillon who not only helped to organize the symposia, but typed the edited manuscripts.

Gary Chamberlain
Patrick J. Howell, S.J.
Seattle University
June, 1990

1

Catholicism and Living Tradition: The Church as a Community of Reception

Michael J. Scanlon, O.S.A.
Washington Theological Union

For many people, Catholicism is a fascinating phenomenon. The range of interest in "the Catholic Thing"[1] includes the superficial journalism of those mystified by the public show of its arcane ritual and the serious interest of those thinkers—Catholic and Protestant—who have explored the "essence," the "ethos," the "genius," etc. of Catholicism as a vital manifestation of Christian faith. A good illustration of the latter is a rather recent study by the Protestant theologian, Langdon Gilkey, entitled *Catholicism Confronts Modernity*.[2] Among the characteristic "marks" describing the Catholic phenomenon Gilkey places "tradition" in the first place: "There is a sense of the reality, the importance, and the 'weight' of tradition and history in the formation of this people and so of her religious truths, religious experience, and human wisdom."[3] Since Gilkey's concern is with Catholicism's ability creatively to adapt itself to the demands of modernity, his choice of "tradition" as the first characteristic of Catholicism is most apposite. For the tradition which has formed this people and continues to form them appears as a "weight" precisely in regard to modernism's identification of tradition as trammel. Immanuel Kant's essay, "What is Enlightenment?" is only the most famous formulation of that modern suspicion of tradition as the enemy of the ideal of autonomy. Accordingly, Catholicism's confrontation with modernity demands that Catholics assume a critical attitude toward their inherited tradition.

This demand for critique of tradition does not have to lead to the assumption of an unrelieved frown on the faces of critical Catholics. The atmosphere has changed today regarding the role of tradition in human life in general. The Enlightenment's intention to overcome tradition by critical thought has been shown to be an uncritical pretension in itself. In our contemporary, "post-modern" world we have come to recognize ourselves as the heirs of unrecognized pathological trends in the Enlightenment's project to place "man on his own" over against the heteronomy of tradition. Indeed, tradition has been "vindicated" in recent reflection.[4] Inherited and critically interpreted, tradition is now understood by many as the matrix of authentic autonomy. But before we explore this contemporary vindication of tradition, let us turn to the emergence of Catholicism in the early Church in an attempt to understand it precisely as a creative answer to the problem of the transmission of the Christian tradition.

Catholicism, Tradition, and Reception

At least since the nineteenth century scholars have been aware of the emergence of "early Catholicism" within the canon of the New Testament.[5] In general terms early Catholicism evinces a concern with order in the church in regard to the conservation of the *fides quae creditur* through orthodoxy, "sound doctrine," the "rule of faith," etc. This concern for the preservation of the apostolic tradition led to the establishment of the hierarchical ministry as "apostolic succession." The structures of the developing "institutional church" were constructed as concrete mediation to assure the transmission of the Christian tradition. From its very inception Catholicism is defined in relation to the tradition which emerged in response to the *hapax* event of salvation: the life, death, and resurrection of Jesus Christ. The issue addressed by early Catholicism was eminently practical: how to provide *media* whereby successive generations of Christians could make contact with the salvific event of Christ which itself as historical event was becoming ever more an event of the past. And the constructs of early Catholicism were (and remain) obviously "practical." Catholicism is Christianity's most concrete and practical way of dealing with the "metaxy" between the anticipation of the *eschaton* in Christ and the still outstanding consummation. As Paul Tillich put it: "Catholicism since the early days of Christianity has step by step eliminated the tremendous tension of the apostolic time, the feeling that we live in the short but decisive period between the first and the second coming of Christ."[6]

For nearly two millennia Catholicism has been the sacramental representation of the memory of Christ to successive generations of Christians.

Tradition, both the process of its transmission and what is being trans-mitted, is identical with the actual life of the Church. The genius of Catholicism is the spontaneous vitality of its "reception" of the tradition through a pneumatically grounded discernment of the "content" of that tradition. *The transmission of the tradition is the act of reception, and it is the act of reception that renders the content of tradition concretely effective or formative of the life of the Church.* "If there is a truth universally acclaimed from early times to Vatican II, it is *that faith and tradition are borne by the whole Church;* that the universal Church is the sole subject, under the sovereignty of the Spirit who has been promised to the Church and who dwells in it."[7]

As the gift of the Spirit in the whole Body of Christ, *reception is a reality of the pneumatic order.* It *resists understanding in terms of neat, logical categories.* It can be described as a communal *phronesis* (a virtue to be explored later in this paper) which guides a pneumatically em-powered communal *praxis* of discipleship. As Yves Congar insists, the no-tion of *reception "derives from a theology of communion,* itself connected with a theology of local churches, a pneumatology and a theology of tradi-tion and a sense of the profound conciliarity of the Church."[8] As Congar makes clear, the notion of reception makes no sense (or becomes pious nonsense) wherever an ecclesiology of communion devolves into an ec-clesiology of hierarchical authoritarianism which recognizes the Holy Spirit as "guarantor of an infallibility of hierarchical courts."[9] Congar's observations concur with those of the Lutheran theologian, Wolfhart Pan-nenberg, who laments the frequent use of the Holy Spirit to legitimate the incomprehensible and the absurd in institutional Christianity, Catholic and Protestant. As Pannenberg puts it:

> This situation only developed in modern times. In the early, and even in the medieval, church, the assertions of the Chris-tian faith convinced people through their substance. It was only when Christianity was forced into a defensive position in modern times that people make a spiritual virtue of necessity, making up what the Christian proclamation lacked in power of conviction by a reference to the Holy Spirit.[10]

Reception is intrinsically linked to the "convincing substance" or to the "content" of the Christian faith. Congar refers to a text from the late 16th century English theologian, Thomas Stapleton, to illustrate the transition from the *tradition* of the whole Church to the office of the *tradens,* (the "official teacher"): "In doctrina fidei non quid dicatur, sed quis loquetur a fideli populo attendendum est."[11]   With this mischievously clear distinction between the *ecclesia docens* (the "teaching church") and the *ecclesia discens* (the "learning church") the criteria for establishing the authentic content of the faith become juridical and the authority of the hierarchical teachers. The ideal of conviction as the result of the proclaimed substance of the gospel cedes to the organizational "ideal" of obedience (that most questionable of all virtues when defined in the superior-subject relationship).[12]

With obvious understatement Congar suggests that "if the *content* of truth and of good is taken into account, the faithful and, better, the *ecclesia,* may be allowed a certain activity of discernment and 'reception'."[13] The authority or effective power of the gospel is *in* the gospel. The gospel does not get its authority from the office of the official preacher or teacher. Formal authority works when it is in possession, i.e., when it is unquestioned because presupposed. But once questioned, all authorities must render an *apologia* to legitimate their claims. In the 19th century Hegel attempted to restore authority to Christianity by explicating the intrinsic intelligibility of its content. He excoriated ecclesiastical "positivism" which substitutes juridical impositions of doctrines and practices for rational understanding. In our own century Karl Rahner rehearsed the Hegelian attempt to display the inherent authority of the content of the gospel with explicit condemnation of the continuing appeals to formal authority. Such appeals are more and more otiose. The oft noted pragmatism of ecclesiastical leaders should realize this fact by now—simply put, it doesn't work! And—to move from a judgment of fact to a judgment of value—it shouldn't work! Appeals to formal authority should heed the practical economy of Ockham's razor!

In keeping with the ethos of Catholicism we must now advance from deconstruction to reconstruction—such is the inexorable optimism of the Catholic experience of grace. If reception describes the Catholic experience of tradition in the contest of a renewed image of the Church as communion, the *magisterium* in the Church has an important role to play. That role is appositely affirmed in the literal meaning of the Greek word for bishop—*episcopos,* overseer. The bishops with the Pope are the "authorities" in the Catholic community. Toward an understanding of their role in the community the thought of the Canadian theologian, Bernard Lonergan, is most enlightening.[14] Lonergan finds no contradiction between the modern ideal of autonomy and the authority of the Catholic tradition. In resonance with Rahner's theology of freedom, with Tillich's notion of theonomy, and with many others, Lonergan contends that the Christian tradition both promotes and sustains authentic autonomy by mediating God's gracious empowerment to overcome the experience of "moral impotency" which accompanies any serious effort toward authentic autonomy. Lonergan describes the path to autonomy in terms of fidelity to self in responding to the exigencies of the inherent dynamism of the human spirit toward self-transcendence. Immanent in the very movement of the human person toward authentic autonomy lie the norms for its achievement. Once these norms have been explicated in Lonergan's "transcendental method," they can take the form of a morality of autonomy in the imperative mood of the "transcendental precepts": be attentive, be intelligent, be reasonable, be responsible. From the realism of the personal quest for autonomy Lonergan extends these norms to the social realm where alone can personal autonomy be realized. In the community authority is legitimate power. This authority lies in the community whose source of power is cooperation, which cooperation has a diachronic and a synchronic dimension. This notion of cooperation is close to what we mean by a living tradition, wherein diachrony and synchrony coincide in that reception which is "the living faith of the dead."[15] Thus, in the Christian community authority lies in the people whose power is that cooperation which is grounded in the pneumatically received tradition in which the faith of those who have gone before us continues to live.

If authority lies in the community, the "authorities" of the community will be those officials to whom certain responsibilities have been entrusted. Just as the authority of the community is legitimate to the extent that the people who constitute the community are authentic, so it is the personal authenticity of the authoritative official which legitimates his or her authority. Authentic authorities enhance the authenticity of their communities in the promotion of the meanings and values of their common tradition by bringing those meanings and values to expression through a process of discernment of what is often referred to as the *sensus fidelium.* Thus, the role of the *magisterium* is most important. As "overseers," the pope and the bishops serve the Church in obedience to the Spirit who inspires the whole community when they articulate the community's lived sense of faith (the *traditio*) whenever and wherever necessary, opportune, or appropriate. When the *magisterium* speaks, what is said gains its "validity" from the correctness of the juridical process followed in accord with the obtaining structures of church order. As Congar admits, "reception is not constitutive of the juridical quality of a decision."[16] It is, however, reception that makes what is said by the *magisterium* concretely *effective* in the life of the Church. The reality of reception characterized the transmission of tradition throughout the first millennium of the existence of the Church—that period when "the Church was understood as a communion of churches."[17] Theologians today speak of reception in terms of the reception of the teachings of Church Councils, the reception of doctrines and practices of a local Church by another Church, and the contemporary receptions of different traditions among the separated Christian communities in the current ecumenical atmosphere. In this paper the reality of reception is explored as a key to the very identity of Catholicism. In short, Catholicism *is* the pneumatic reception of the apostolic *paradosis*. One way to bring out the distinctiveness of Catholicism in regard to the transmission of the Christian tradition is to contrast it with the Protestant understanding. In language reminiscent of Tillich we might say that if the "material element" in Protestantism is *sola gratia* and the "formal element" is *sola scriptura*, the "material element" in Catholicism is the immanence of grace and the "formal element" is reception. To overcome the impression that Catholicism is an authoritarian religion (an impression unfortunately promoted by the excessively hierarchical ecclesiology of Catholicism's second millennium) and to recover the authentic Catholicism of pneumatic communion (always present during the second millennium but at times muted) we must more reflectively appropriate what we spontaneously do under the inspiration of the Spirit of Christ. We must achieve what might be called the specifically Catholic form of Paul Ricoeur's "second naïveté."[18]

The path to this critical faith is hermeneutics. Just as "historical consciousness" means that people always produced their own history, but now we know that, so "hermeneutical consciousness" alerts us to the fact that Catholicism has always been the pneumatic reception of tradition, but now we know that. If historical consciousness intensifies our awareness of human freedom and so our responsibility for its consequences, so a "hermeneutics of reception" should intensify our attunement to the Spirit who is the nourishing matrix of all authentic freedom.

Toward a Hermeneutics of Reception

In the past two decades Catholic theology in this country has experienced a series of significant "shifts" or "turns." The pervasive influence of Karl Rahner and Bernard Lonergan witnesses to the theological renaissance that followed Catholic theology's (rather late!) "turn to the subject." Rahner's transcendental theology became the classic mystagogy of the century. Lonergan's "transcendental method" articulated the "basic anthropological component" (self-appropriated *praxis*) for all theology. In a short time this "turn to the subject" was complemented by the "socio-political turn" (from the *praxis* of subjectivity to the *praxis* of intersubjectivity) of the European political theologies, the Latin American liberation theologies, and feminist, black, and Hispanic-American theologies—all still developing. The third turn is the "linguistic turn" wherein hermeneutics becomes the all-encompassing path to truth.[19] Properly understood, this turn does not negate but rather intends to sublate the advances of the earlier turns. Correcting the "turn to the subject," the linguistic turn insists that there is not a historical or non-linguistic subject. Enhancing the pragmatic concerns of the socio-political turn, the linguistic turn reveals the intrinsic connection between speech and both ethics and politics.[20]

As they attempt to understand understanding in terms of "the conversation that we are," theologians today are in dialogue with the modern hermeneutical tradition from Schleiermacher and Dilthey to Heidegger, Gadamer, Wittgenstein, Habermas, and Ricoeur. Of these thinkers I choose Gadamer as the one whose contributions to a hermeneutic of reception are particularly valuable. In his great work, *Truth and Method,* Gadamer presents a compelling vindication of tradition over against what he criticizes as the Enlightenment's "prejudice against prejudice."[21] In his attempts to rehabilitate the realities of tradition and authority Gadamer is a natural dialogue partner for a Catholic who seeks the critical retrieval of authentic Catholicism. For Gadamer tradition is not inherited heteronomy, and its authority is not the violence of authoritarianism.

Against all modern forms of subjectivism as well as against all forms of reductionistic positivism Gadamer claims that understanding is not to be understood as an activity of the subject; it is, rather, a "happening," an "event," a "*pathos*."[22] Understanding is not *an* activity alongside other activities. It is universal—it pervades all activities. Gadamer's insistence on the universality of understanding is reminiscent of the universalism which inspires Lonergan's "transcendental method." But the latter presents this "method" as the ahistorical "rock" which is the condition for the possibility for all history and culture.[23] For Lonergan "understanding" is the second level of authentic self-enactment, a level which forms part of the noetic dynamism of the human spirit in a movement toward authentic *praxis.*

Between understanding and decision lies the all-important level of judgment without which there is no knowing the truth. For Gadamer, however, understanding is the all-embracing description of human *praxis*. It is neither ahistorical nor merely noetic. Gadamer's point of departure is the human person as always already formed and shaped by the intrinsically linguistic power of tradition. Against Enlightenment's enthronement of the ideal of a transcultural reason, Gadamer insists that "It is not so much our judgments as our prejudices that constitute our being."[24] Some of our prejudices are blind and thus unproductive; but others are "enabling." The latter prejudices empower us to move into the process of understanding. It is within the process of understanding the tradition that we will be able to distinguish between blind and enabling prejudices.

Obvious in Gadamer's description of the process of understanding is the influence of Heidegger. The initiative passes from the interpreter to the reality being interpreted. Here Gadamer uses his famous analogy of "play." In the event of play "the structure of play absorbs the player into itself, and thus takes from him the burden of the initiative, which constitutes the actual strain of existence."[25] Like play, understanding is a "happening." Meaning is not "mental"—it is realized only in and through the event of understanding. Tradition carries its own authority when we allow it to "speak to us." But here "authority has nothing to do with obedience, but rather with knowledge."[26] This "conversation" with the tradition is in principle always an open-ended process; it must be resumed anew as long as history remains what it is—an unfinished process of humanity in the making. As our horizons change, so will the tradition speak to us in different ways—*if* we continue to acknowledge the claim to authority which the tradition asserts.

For Gadamer understanding is incomplete until that moment is reached which he calls "application." Here is human "interest" in the emancipatory possibilities of the tradition in which we stand. Here is the "point" behind what seems to be another chapter in the history of philosophy's attempt merely to "interpret" the world, when the point is to *change* it! Gadamer is obviously aware of the indictment of philosophy as mere interpretation in Marx's "Eleventh Thesis on Feuerbach." He accepts the contemporary insistence of all those who have made "the praxiological turn" that not only is theory not higher than *praxis* but that *praxis* is the whence and whither of theory. The moment of "application" is the heart of hermeneutics. Understanding is eminently practical, for it is the personal appropriation of the fact that we are the products of the "effective history" of our tradition.

We "belong" to a tradition—here the Christian tradition—from whose origins we are distant by almost two thousand years but whose historical efficacy has been carried forward through the centuries by the thought and experience of generations of Christians who have received and transmitted the same tradition. For each generation—as for us—the "horizon of reception" is limited by the concrete historical situation, but each historical horizon is open both to reception and further enrichment of the inherited tradition. For Gadamer understanding does not come from a romantic rehearsing of the horizons of the past but from the search for a "fusion of horizons," wherein our prejudices are tested as new possibilities for personal and communal living are revealed.

It is important for our purposes to repeat that "application" is the central moment in the process of understanding the tradition. Application is not "applied theory." To underscore this point Gadamer insists that application is the moment when hermeneutics is fused with what Aristotle called *phronesis*. *Phronesis* is the virtue which enlightens ethical and political *praxis*. It is the spontaneous, quasi-instinctual ability to discern the right thing to be done in the changeable circumstances of life. It is a moral "know how" that results from experience and reflection, and it is sustained and promoted within a community of shared moral norms and principles. For Gadamer's hermeneutics is the contemporary form of Aristotle's practical philosophy. Understanding as application is a form of *phronesis*. Belonging to a tradition forms people by its linguistic mediation of meaning in that process of understanding by which application as *phronesis* guides *praxis*.

For further clarification of Gadamer's retrieval of the Aristotelian virtue of *phronesis* Lonergan's "transcendental method" is most helpful. This method of authentic self-enactment is the path to both personal and communal *phronesis*. Sustained fidelity to Lonergan's "transcendental precepts" produces the *phronemos* (the prudent person). *Phronesis* guides *praxis*, but *phronesis* itself is the fruit of "phronetic" *praxis*.

Gadamer's emphasis on the intersubjective or communal setting for the realization of application as *phronesis* is further developed by the "hermeneutics of reception" elaborated by his student, Hans Robert Jauss.[27] Jauss represents "literary history" as a "challenge" to "literary theory." His notion of "literary history" is akin to our concern with the relationship between Catholicism and tradition. For Jauss every literary work is received over against a contemporary "horizon of expectation." Ordinary works are in harmony with the given horizon of expectation, and their concordance with this horizon renders them "ordinary"—they please and entertain for a time. But great works (Gadamer's "classics") are always in tension with the given horizon of expectation. They confound and even negate the given horizon. They demand the formation of new horizons in order to become intelligible. With the establishment of these new horizons of reception, however, the great works tend to become domesticated. Their original negativity over against their original horizon of expectation is forgotten, and their formative power in relation to new possibilities for life is diminished. Jauss is convinced that Gadamer's presentation of the classic as somehow timelessly relevant in its own constant mediation describes the cultural domestication of the great work and conceals its original power of negation. For Jauss the classic must confound contemporary horizons of expectation to remain a classic. The great work must continue to demand further expansions of horizons in order really to "work," i.e., to perform its "emancipatory social or perpetually formative function."[28]

Jauss' hermeneutics of reception invites us to reflect on the "effective history" of tradition with attention to the diachronic "concretizations" of its influence. The linguistic power of tradition is the result, not of its autonomous existence, but of the interaction of what is transmitted and how it is received by the people. The vitality of a tradition is inconceivable without the active participation of its addressees. Reception is "an energy formative of history."[29] The history of Christianity is the successive "fusions of horizons" of past and present as the meaning embedded in its tradition is actualized in new events of critical reception by successive generations of believers. Just as early Catholicism was the creative reception of the early Christian tradition over against the disappointed horizon of expectation of an imminent *parousia,* so contemporary Catholicism evinces a dynamic reception of the tradition over against the disappointed horizon of immanent progress in history.[30]

Catholicism as a Classic

During the nineteenth century Christian theologians became interested in exploring the "essence" of Catholicism (and the "essence" of Protestantism as well).[31] The Catholic Tübingen theologian, Adam Mohler, identified Catholicism as "the form of Christianity that fully accepts the incarnation."[32] From this full acceptance follows a "high" ecclesiology: "The visible Church is the Son of God himself, everlasting by manifesting himself among men in a human form, perpetually renovated, and eternally young—the permanent incarnation of the same, as in Holy Writ, even the faithful are called the Body of Christ."[33] This discernment of continuities is a distinctive trait of the Catholic imagination. It is classically illustrated in the Catholic theology of nature and grace. The Biblical teaching on the intrinsic relationship between redemption and creation is the basis for the distinctively Catholic vision of fundamental continuity between nature and grace. If grace is the fulfillment of nature, and if the natural is always attuned to the supernatural (as in Aquinas), the nothing is merely "profane." For the sacramental imagination which results anyone or anything in creation can become a bearer of the sacred. This accent on continuity between nature and grace has often led observers of the Catholic phenomenon to note (with both positive and negative evaluations) its "naturalness," or even its "paganism."[34]

The so-called Modernists at the turn of this century were energized in their theological efforts by a vision of the impelling beauty of authentic Catholicism.[35] They sought to restore the intrinsic authority of the Catholic faith over against the excessively rigid hierarchical authoritarianism of their day. With prior and later theologians they recognized the emphasis on divine immanence throughout the Catholic tradition from the Greek patristic theology of grace as "divinization," to Augustine's theology of "operating" and "cooperating" grace, to Thomas Aquinas' theology of grace as the permanent elevation of the soul to parity with God, to the Tridentine teaching on the real, internal renewal of the justified person, to "the world of grace" which is the theology of Karl Rahner.

The Modernists also attempted to overcome the static conceptualism of Neo-Scholastic theology by promoting a new sensitivity to the primarily symbolic nature of religious language. But the reigning conceptualists of the time immediately read into the word, symbolic, the invidious adverbs "merely," or "just"! For them symbolic discourse was "merely symbolic" in the sense that it connoted "subjectivism" over against the "hard objectivity" of concepts. Again, the insights of the Modernists were rendered abortive by hierarchical condemnation. In recent theology, informed as it is by conversation with hermeneutical philosophy, the role of symbol in religious language has received its due prominence. Symbol is now understood as *the way* in which the hidden depths of reality are disclosed. If *the* hidden death of all reality, of all history is the divine immanence, then the primary revelation of that pervasive depth is the symbol. For any religious tradition certain symbols are central keys to the whole symbolic system. For Israel, the central symbols were Exodus and Covenant. For Judaism the focal symbol was the Torah. For Jesus the core symbol was the Kingdom of God. For Christians the central symbol is Jesus Christ (with special focus in our time on Jesus). These symbols become effective when they create the consciousness or mindset of Christian disciples. This powerful understanding of the efficacy of symbols is attributed by Gregory Baum to Hegel.[36]

Baum clarifies this meaning of symbol through Paul Ricoeur's distinction between "that which" and "that through which"—the symbols, Covenant, Torah, Kingdom of God, Jesus, would be "that which;" as effectively received by believers these symbols become "that through which."[37] Living tradition, the lived sense of faith of the Christian community, is nicely clarified by this "Hegelian" understanding of the efficacy of symbols in the constitution of human consciousness. The tradition is vital insofar as the disciples of Jesus perceive, understand, and evaluate reality through the symbol, Jesus.

There is yet another meaning of symbol that is extremely important for Catholicism. This meaning is derived by Baum from Marx. To Hegel's insight that consciousness creates the social structures of history Marx puts a "semi-colon." It is also true according to Marx that social structures create human consciousness. Thus, symbols are the reflection of society in consciousness. Accordingly, as Catholics are socialized in the community of the Church, their mindsets are formed by the concrete ways the gospel is embodied in the structures of the Church. The symbolic structures of the Church should support the proclamation of the revealed symbols which are intended to construct the imaginations of the faithful. But contradictions may arise between the gospel proclaimed and the gospel embodied in the structures of the Church—a point which raises the question: Which is more effective, the gospel proclaimed or the gospel embodied? Catholicism has always placed its emphasis on the latter as providing the media for the reception of the tradition of grace. To remain faithful to its own "genius": contemporary Catholicism must face the question of the "symbolic adequacy" of its visible structures.[38]

Catholicism remains a "classic" interpretation of the Christian faith.[39] By its very density it claims attention, and it has claimed much "attention" of late! This paper has attempted to make a case for the thesis that "reception" is a key to understanding the vitality of Catholicism through the centuries. There is something of the "transcendental" about this approach—it has tried to name what we as Catholics have always done spontaneously. Need for reflection on the tacit presuppositions of our spontaneous performance is a part of our present situation. We have passed from the days of "speculative" theology to the demands for "critical" theology wherein we try to uncover what has always been the dynamic principle behind our historical practice. Throughout the centuries of our common "primary naïveté" we have pneumatically received the tradition. Today we must reflect on our "performance," because we know that the "pragmatics" of our religious symbols has consequences beyond our explicit intentions. As Catholics, we can name our deepest "presupposition" as the immanence of grace, a salvific presence which has become efficacious for us as the symbols of the tradition formed our imagination, empowering us for discipleship. In light of naming this source and principle we have become uneasy with what Walter Kasper has described as the situation of the Church in our day. Kasper has acutely observed the fact that the "extraordinary powers" of the ecclesiastical authorities, to be employed when "the normal forms of communication do not function," have become the ordinary *modus operandi*—thus, "in practice in the Church we live with a permanent suspension of the constitution:"

> In the normal situation the magisterium should . . . adhere to the proper forms for collective and collegial (conciliar and synodal) discovery of the truth. This could only benefit its authority in a crisis. Otherwise the sword could easily be found blunt when it was really needed.[40]

Catholicism as "a community of reception" is becoming aware of itself. In accord with its own "classical form of religious expression," *manifestation,* it seeks symbolic adequacy as a world communion of "dialogical communities."[41] As it becomes itself more and more the catholic manifestation of universal grace, its "receptive instinct" will inform its ever expanding "living tradition." "For reality, when it includes human beings, is no longer that which it is, but also everything that is mission in it, everything that it must still become."[42]

Notes

1. Cf. Rosemary Haughton, *The Catholic Thing* (Springfield, IL: Templegate Publishers, 1979).

2. New York: The Seabury Press, 1975.

3. *Ibid.* p. 17.

4. Cf. Jaroslav Pelikan, *The Vindication of Tradition* (New Haven: Yale University Press, 1984).

5. Cf. John Elliot, "A Catholic Gospel: Reflections on 'Early Catholicism' in the New Testament," *Catholic Biblical Quarterly* 31 (1969) 213-223.

6. Paul Tillich, "The Permanent Significance of the Catholic Church for Protestantism," *The Protestant Digest* 3 (1941) 24.

7. Yves Congar, "Reception as an Ecclesiology Reality" in Guiseppe Alberigo & Anton Weiler, eds., *Election and Consensus in the Church* Concilium 77 (New York: Herder & Herder, 1972), p. 54.

8. *Ibid.,* p. 60.

9. *Ibid.,* p. 60.

10. Wolfhart Pannenburg, *The Apostles' Creed* (Philadelphia: Westminster Press, 1972), p. 130.

11. Congar, *op. cit.,* p. 61: "In the doctrine of the faith the people must attend not to what is said but to who shall speak." This illustration from the late sixteenth century of the primacy of formal authority should not be understood as the beginning of the modern tendency. In his fascinating study of the early development of Roman claims to exceptional authority (the "Janus complex of tradition and discretion") Karl Morrison quotes the fifth century Pope Celestine I: "The people must be taught, not followed." Cf. Morrison, *Tradition and Authority in the Western Church 300-1140* (Princeton: Princeton University Press, 1969), p. 87.

12. Cf. Nicholas Lash, *Voices of Authority* (Shepherdstown, WV: Patmos Press, 1976), pp. 101-16.

13. Congar, *op. cit.,* p. 61.

14. For what follows cf. Bernard Lonergan, "Dialectic of Authority" in Frederick Crowe, ed., *A Third Collection* (New York: Paulist Press, 1985).

15. Jaroslav Pelikan, *op. cit.,* p. 65; for Pelikan's own "evangelical catholicity" cf. his *Obedient Rebels: Catholic Substance and Protestant Principle in Luther's Reformation* (New York: Harper & Row, 1964).

16. Congar, *op. cit.,* p. 66.

17. Thomas Rausch, "Reception Past and Present," *Theological Studies* 47 (September, 1986), 500.

18. Paul Ricoeur, *Symbolism of Evil,* (Boston: Beacon Press, 1969), pp. 351-57.

19. Cf. *Proceedings of the Forty-Second Annual Convention of the Catholic Theological Society of America 1987* (Volume 42).

20. Cf. Fred Dallmayr, *Language and Politics* (Notre Dame: University of Notre Dame Press, 1984); for the connection between the linguistic turn and ethics cf. Anne Patrick, "The Linguistic Turn and Moral Theology," C.T.S.A. *Proceedings.*, Vol. 42, pp. 38-56.

21. Hans-Georg Gadamer, *Truth and Method* (New York: Crossroad, 1982).

22. Bernard Lonergan, *Method in Theology* (New York: Herder & Herder, 1972), p. 19.

23. Cf. Richard Bernstein, *Beyond Objectivism and Relativism: Science, Hermeneutics and Praxis* (Philadelphia: University of Pennsylvania Press, 1983), pp. 109-50.

24. Gadamer, "The Universality of the Hermeneutical Problem," *Philosophical Hermeneutics,* (Berkeley: University of California Press, 1976), p. 9.

25. Bernstein, p. 114.

26. *Ibid.,* p. 129.

27. Cf. Jauss, "Literary History as a Challenge to Literary Theory," *Toward an Aesthetic of Reception* (Minneapolis: University of Minnesota Press, 1982), pp. 3-45.

28. *Ibid,* p. 10.

29. *Ibid.,* p. 19.

30. A clear example of dynamic reception in contemporary Catholicism is the new concern with social justice, peace, liberation, etc.

31. Cf. Avery Dulles, "The Essence of Catholicism: Protestant and Catholic Perspectives," *The Thomist* 48, 4 (October 1984) 607-33.

32. *Ibid.,* p. 617.

33. *Ibid.,* p. 617.

34. Cf. George Tyrrell, "Reflections on Catholicism," *Through Scylla and Charybdis* (London: Longmans, Green, 1907), pp. 20-84; David Tracy, *The Analogical Imagination* (New York: Crossroad, 1981), p. 217.

35. Cf. Gabriel Daly, *Transcendence and Immanence: A Study in Catholic Modernism and Integralism* (Oxford: Clarendon Press, 1980); for a good illustration of the Modernist interest in Catholicism cf. Ellen Leonard, *George Tyrrell and the Catholic Tradition* (New York: Paulist Press, 1982.

36. Gregory Baum, *Religion and Alienation* (New York: Paulist Press, 1975), pp. 240-41.

37. *Ibid.,* p. 243.

38. In his presentation of the "Marxist" sense of symbol Baum refers to Talcott Parson's notion of "symbolic adequacy;" *Ibid.*, p. 249.

39. Cf. Stephen Happel and David Tracy, *A Catholic Vision* (Philadelphia: Fortress Press, 1980), pp. 3-4.

40. Walter Kasper, *An Introduction to Christian Faith* (New York: Paulist Press, 1980), p. 149.

41. For "manifestation" as the classic form of Catholic religious expression cf. David Tracy, *The Analogical Imagination,* pp. 202-18; for the ideal of a "dialogical community" for the promotion of *phronesis* cf. Richard Bernstein, *op. cit.*, p. 159.

42. Jauss, *op. cit.*, p. 15.

2

Authority, Women, and Church: Reconsidering the Relationship

Anne E. Patrick, S.N.J.M.
Carleton College

The subject of authority in the church is a thoroughly ethical matter, for it involves the question of right relationships, and matters of justice and injustice. Simply because as Catholics we affirm the sacramentality of the church does not mean that ecclesiology should be a value-free branch of theology, untouched by the insights of Christian moral wisdom. Instead ethics needs to work with other theological disciplines on the questions of authority, episcopacy, and primacy, asking how we may serve our common needs for unity, order, and leadership in a way that respects two insights that are having a profound impact on the moral and religious lives of believers today: a growing conviction of the fundamental equality of women and men, and a deepening appreciation of the fact that God's Spirit is given to all the faithful and not only to those in positions of hierarchical office.

In fact, the topic of church authority is much more closely related to the movement for justice for women than is generally recognized. The recent cases concerning "authority and dissent" in the church, such as those of Professor Charles Curran, Archbishop Raymond Hunthausen, and the women religious known as the "Vatican 24," are symptoms of a conflict well underway between two competing sets of ideals for the Christian life, each of which understands religious authority and what it means to be a "good Catholic" differently. The differences may be sketched in terms of two paradigms, the longstanding "patriarchal" one, and a newer one, which may be termed "egalitarian" or "feminist."[1] Whereas the older view regards spirituality as a matter between the "soul" and God, the newer view emphasizes that God is immanent in all relationships. It understands

God's relation to creation not as one of domination and control, but rather as one of energizing and nurturance. The patriarchal model was shaped by otherworldliness, by patterns of domination and subordination, and by the misogynism and body-rejecting dualism long part of western culture. In contrast, the newer model understands reason itself to be embodied, and women and men to be equal partners in the human community. Instead of stressing authoritarian *control* over passions and those who are subordinate, the emphasis is on *respect* and mutuality. In this view, authority influences, inspires, and coordinates various gifts; it does not coerce.

Some are beginning to see connections between what women typically experience in patriarchal society and what layfolk, priests, and bishops sometimes suffer at the hands of domineering religious authorities. The model of domination and subordination that is at the heart of patriarchy expresses itself most clearly in unjust relations between males and females, but it is also seen in many other sorts of unjust relationships. By the same token, a model of mutuality and respect has implications for healing relationships not only between women and men but also between the Christian communities and their religious leaders.

Perhaps one of the greatest gifts the women's movement for justice has brought to the church is the clear recognition that whatever may be true about the catechism description of the church as a "perfect society," the phrase cannot mean what complacent Catholics used to believe that it meant. One of the problems of our tradition's emphasis on the sacramentality of the religious institution, on the fact that grace is indeed mediated through the society we call "church," has been the tendency to exempt this society from the ethical scrutiny given to other societies. Some have mistakenly held to an ecclesiology that stresses a view of divine foundation and guidance to the point where the human, and indeed the sinful aspects of the church are not recognized and properly addressed. The situation is parallel to the one where believers are reluctant to apply the techniques of literary and historical criticism to biblical texts. The result in both cases can be a style of faith that confuses God with human realities mediating God's presence, in other words, the classic temptation of idolatry.[2]

If Protestants have sometimes succumbed to "bibliolatry," the recurrent temptation for Catholics has been "ecclesiolatry," and the corrective we need is not a rejection of the church or legitimate ecclesiastical authority, but rather a realistic recognition of the humanity of the church, which entails that leaders and other members be responsible for the quality of its life and the cogency of its witness. A glance at history confirms that issues of power and justice are sooner or later involved whenever two or three are gathered together in Jesus' name. The fact that we are concerned with an institution with special ties to the sacred does not dispense us from our basic obligation to strive in all contexts of our lives to discern "what God is enabling and requiring" us to be and to do, as James M. Gustafson has so aptly described the task of Christian ethics.[3]

There are many questions that need to be addressed once the decision is made to draw the ethical implications of accepting the "true humanity" of the church. In what follows I shall focus on a single one of these, namely the question of what God seems to be enabling and requiring Catholic women to be and to do in relation to the church at this juncture of its history. Although the relevance of this question to the topics of authority, primacy, and episcopacy may not be immediately apparent, there is no doubt that women's decisions about church membership and involvement are greatly affecting the religious institution and its leaders, and one has every reason to think the effects will be more and more striking as time goes on.

It is relevant to present and future church leaders that women today are experiencing alienation, often profound alienation, from the religious tradition that once gave meaning to their lives. One might paraphrase a famous remark of the nineteenth-century Anglican churchman Matthew Arnold. Responding to the intellectual tensions of his day, Arnold observed: "At the present moment two things about the Christian religion must surely be clear to anybody with eyes in his head. One is, that men cannot do without it; the other, that they cannot do with it as it is."[4] Arnold's first premise has been discredited, and we must amend his second point to something like, "Whether or not modern persons can do without the church, most *women* cannot do with it as it is." Arnold was right to see how urgent it was to adapt to the changed *intellectual* climate of the nineteenth century, and it is equally urgent today for the tradition to adapt to the changed *moral* climate of the twentieth century, a climate that takes for granted the full human dignity of females, and assumes that women and men are radically equal in their humanity. As Margaret Farley has pointed out, we are living in an era when "profound conceptual and symbolic shifts have occurred in relation to gender differentiation and sex roles. Indeed, so profound are these changes and so far-reaching their consequences that one is tempted to say that they are to the moral life of persons what the Copernican revolution was to science or what the shift to the subject was to philosophy."[5]

To appreciate the significance of this change in moral climate, we may find it useful to call on metaphor, and to think of the cultural transition now in progress as the ending of a sexist ice age. Recalling what the retreat of the glacier that once covered part of this country has meant for the upper midwest will give us an analogue for grasping what the end of religiously legitimated sexism will entail for Christianity.

The ice age metaphor has the merit of helping us realize the scope of the changes involved, but it can be misleading if we imagine that the transition from the old order of injustice between the sexes to a new order of equality and mutuality is an inevitable natural event. Rather we have here an *ethical task* for all who recognize the truth of the new vision. Moral theologians wisely stress that the first step in discerning moral obligation is to get a picture of the situation calling for a moral response. In other words, we need to *interpret* what is going on before we can prudently decide what we should be doing about it.

The Situation of Oppression

When we focus on the question "What is going on with respect to women and the church?", the answers are multiple and complex. But one thing remains true: even today, *oppression* is going on. Across the board females continue to suffer unjust discrimination on the basis of sex. The degrees and forms of this sexism vary widely, but a good deal of it remains even in the dioceses and local congregations known generally for their liberalism. Nor should this be altogether surprising, for patriarchy has held sway in our culture for millennia, and removing its influence from our structures and our psyches is not something that can be done overnight. By patriarchy I mean a social system biased in favor of maleness, which tends to absolutize male authority and to privilege the class of ruling males.[6] Moreover, patriarchy has been religiously legitimated in Christianity by an overwhelming bias in favor of masculine imagery for the deity. The child named Sylvia was surely on to something when she wrote in a letter, "Dear God. Are boys better than girls? I know you are one, but try to be fair."[7]

It is now more than twenty years since Mary Daly's first book, *The Church and the Second Sex,* called attention to injustice toward women in the church, and since then efforts have been made, both feeble and strenuous, to mitigate this injustice. And because change *has* occurred in these last two decades, many are puzzled that the pressure for change continues to mount despite the improvements that have occurred. To understand why this is the case, it helps to recognize that oppression is not a quantitative phenomenon.

The essence of oppression is not the fact that, say, three hundred unfair things are being done to an oppressed group, so that if twenty-five or fifty, or even two hundred and fifty of these practices were stopped things would really be better. True, things might *feel* better in a lot of ways. But the very fact that the number of unfair practices is reduced highlights the injustices that remain. The partial remedies make the oppressed wonder all the more, "Why are things this way?"

Instead of seeing oppression as simply a collection of unfair practices, it is better to view it in religious terms. Essentially oppression involves a situation where human beings attempt to play God over other human beings. They do this by defining the meaning and purpose of others' lives without respect for the mystery that is basic to human personhood. This is the first stage in what may be termed the process of oppression. The second occurs when those whose lives are defined *internalize* the oppressor's judgment of their purpose and worth. In other words, there are both objective and subjective dimensions to oppression—factors outside the self, and factors within. Psychological oppression is harder to document than the grosser forms of physical oppression, such as slavery or the laws of apartheid, but in both forms the mystery and worth of a person are violated by an oppressor's attempting to define what someone else is good for, and not good for. It matters little whether this is done in harsh tones, or in gentler ones, such as by invoking theories of "woman's special nature" or "the feminine role in God's plan." The violation of personhood by others' powers of definition is the issue. Nor should we fail to recognize that there does not have to be someone deliberately causing *or* acquiescing to the oppression if the social and mental structures of domination and subordination are in place. For the terrible thing about oppression is that once it is internalized, it perpetuates itself without need of deliberate decision or physical force.[8]

In the last 20 years *awareness* about sexism in church and society has spread at a phenomenal rate. Women and men alike are experiencing more and more conflict between their ideals of equality and the discriminatory reality they encounter in worship and other dimensions of church life. And these new perceptions have yielded a range of responses to the new consciousness. Many deserve praise for the ways they have worked to overcome sexism in the churches. One thinks of those who first risked welcoming women to the seminaries and later to the pulpits and governing bodies of various Protestant denominations. One thinks of those Roman Catholic priests who signed their names to the charter of Priests for Equality, thereby dissenting publicly from official Vatican teaching on women's ordination, and insuring that they will not soon be called to serve as bishops.

It is crucial, however, not to limit attention to the responses of those already in power in the church, who are still exclusively male, but instead to attend to the responses of *women* to their growing awareness of being connected by ties of faith to an institution that has been a major culprit in our oppression. I am interested in asking: what is correct "church practice" for female moral agents in view of the institutionalized injustice toward women in Catholicism? What is God enabling and requiring *us* to be and to do?

A Map of Women's Responses to Ecclesial Oppression

To approach this question we might begin by considering several types of responses that women are making to the church today. It is useful, in fact, to analyze the relationship between "women" and "church" as a contemporary case of the recurring debate within the Christian tradition that theologian H. Richard Niebuhr probed in his classic study of 1951, *Christ and Culture*. I am suggesting that the same dynamics Niebuhr found in the tension between Christ and culture, or between the gospel and the social environment in which it is lived, are also present in the tension we see today between women and the church.

In applying Niebuhr's method to a problem he did not address, I shall use the term "church" in a restricted sense, namely that of historical religious institution. It is perhaps more problematic to exchange the first term of Niebuhr's pair, "Christ," for that of "women," than it is to say that the church represents a cultural entity, but there is precedent in such doctrines as the Mystical Body of Christ and in biblical texts such as "Where two or three are gathered in my name . . ." (Matt. 18:20) for an analysis that stresses the identification of Christ and Christian. Niebuhr himself said that the title *Christ and Culture* is a shorthand phrase expressing a recurrent dilemma within the tradition, a debate that has been formulated in a wide variety of terms in the past. He mentions, for example, the relations of Protestantism and capitalism, or Pietism and nationalism, among others. In our day the recurrent debate includes the dialectic between "women" and "church."[9]

As Niebuhr reminds us, the "method of typology" is "historically inadequate," which is to say that the categories are useful as an aid to thinking but should not be applied rigidly to data that is far more complex than any heuristic tool can accommodate.[10] No typology or "map" can capture the rich variety of life, but, if properly understood, a typology can help to orient those who are searching for answers to ethical questions. We may profitably adapt his typology of responses to the "Christ and culture" tension as a heuristic aid for assessing a confusing contemporary scene. All five of Niebuhr's categories—1) Christ of culture, 2) Christ against culture, 3) Christ above culture, 4) Christ and culture in paradox, and 5) Christ transforming culture—are useful for answering the question of what is going on with respect to women and the churches. Moreover, the fifth model, which Niebuhr called "transformationist," provides what I consider an ideal answer to the question of what *should* be going on. In other words, women are transforming the churches, and to the extent that their energy for reform represents the values of love, truth, and justice, they ought indeed to be doing so.

One of the reasons the map of types of responses cannot do full justice to the complexities involved is that women are never simply "women" in general. Besides being female a woman also belongs to an age group, a racial/ethnic group, and a social/economic class. She lives in a certain geographic region and a certain neighborhood within that region. She works at home or in various other places, or more likely, in both. And her life is colored by all sorts of relationships, including her relationship to a particular denomination. However useful our model may be, we still need to keep in mind that the concrete reality of women is much more complex than the abstraction "women" suggests.

Furthermore, a full analysis would need to attend to the enormous variety on the "church" side of the relationship, noting, for example, the vast differences among Catholic dioceses as well as among parishes within each diocese. And beyond this, a really complete analysis would require substantial empirical research. Some valuable studies have been published, including the research on Protestant women clergy by Carroll, Hargrove, and Lummis, as well as the volume *Angry Catholic Women* by Greeley and Durkin.[11] All of this having been said, the abstract model can shed light on our experience, and it is to this model of five ways in which women are relating to the church that I now turn.

Type 1: Women Content with the Church

In the first place, we know there are women for whom the term *agreement* best captures their unquestioning relationship with patriarchal Christian culture. Although their numbers are shrinking dramatically, many can still be called "Women Content with the Church." While a feminist analysis would speak of their internalized oppression, the women themselves do not see things this way. Rather, they feel comfortable with their subordinate role, they find feminist complaints ridiculous or threatening, and they are honored to be of service to patriarchal authority, which they associate with divinity. Because of their willingness to serve in token capacity on boards and committees and because of their predictable subservience to male authority, such women are hindrances to the reform agenda. It is difficult for feminist women to be patient with their sisters who see things this way, but it ought to be admitted that many feminists once felt fairly comfortable themselves in the patriarchal religious culture.[12]

Type 2: Women Against the Church

The dissonance experienced when women discover the gap between Christian ideals of love and justice and the sexism of Christian theology and Church practice is often too great to be endured. Nearly two decades ago the president of Church Women United in a major city told me that in her Presbyterian congregation the study group on women in the Bible was the quickest exit route from the church for some. It is not surprising that women once loyal to the church do an about-face when they apprehend the magnitude of Christian patriarchy's betrayal of gospel ideals.

The second model, that of *opposition*, or "Women Against the Church," expresses their alienation well. Such opposition is evident in the anger of formerly Christian women who have abandoned the church for NOW groups or who seek to develop their spirituality exclusively in neopagan or postchristian feminist communities. Instead of bringing hot dishes to church suppers, such women now answer rape crisis hotlines. It is no exaggeration to say that some of these alienated women now regard the faith they once cherished to be a form of blindness or even a destructive addiction akin to alcoholism. One hears now and then the phrase "recovering Catholic" as an expression of such feelings. If Marabel Morgan's book

Total Woman represents the first model, that of agreement, the later Mary Daly is surely the prime spokeswoman for this second model, that of opposition. Daly in fact names this response well in the title "Sisterhood as Anti-Church," which she gives to a chapter in her second book, *Beyond God the Father*.[13] Tertullian's famous question from the third century, "What has Athens to do with Jerusalem?", has been reformulated as "What have women to do with Vatican City?", and answered with a resounding, "Women who respect themselves should have *nothing* to do with the oppressive patriarchal institutions of Christianity."

Exactly how many women have totally rejected the church is difficult to know, but we can be sure there are quite a few, and their numbers are growing. In a volume he wrote with his sister, Mary Greeley Durkin, Andrew Greeley estimated that as of 1984 between one million and a million and a half Catholic women of all ages did not attend church regularly because of a "complex interplay of imagery" regarding God, Woman, Mother, and Church. He also found emphasis on gender roles a significant factor in the non-attendance of some 200,000 young Catholic men.[14]

As with Niebuhr's original typology, my first two categories—agreement and opposition, or, "Women Content with the Church" and "Women Against the Church"—represent opposite extremes. Those who see perfect consonance between their womanhood and the church value the tradition uncritically and reject out of hand the feminist critique of religious patriarchy. The "women against the church," by contrast, embrace feminism and reject Christianity with equal force. The remaining three categories differ from these first two in that they are centrist positions, which accept some elements of both sides of the polarity. That is, they see some validity in the tradition as well as in the feminist critique. Where they differ is in how they respond to the tension.

Type 3: Women Above the Church

This response can be envisioned as the "feminist spiritual community on a pedestal." There is a romantic and sectarian quality to this response. Women who believe the Christian gospel is meaningful and liberating, but whose experience within actual Christian communities has been oppressive, may well opt for a solution whereby a strain of Christian feminism becomes the "new church" for them. Having been nurtured in traditional patriarchal Christianity, they leave their former churches behind, but not in total angry rejection. Rather, the old religious affiliations are simply cast off like outgrown, constricting garments, and a new circle of worship and discussion celebrates the liberation its members experience from the old ways of internal and external oppression. What distinguishes this romantic sectarian model is the tendency to add feminism on top of the Christian heritage and then to exist as comfortably as possible on the summit, without concern for the ambiguous structures of mainline Christianity below, which are regularly experienced by the unenlightened.

Type 4: Women and Church in Paradox

The fourth model involves holding contradictory allegiances to the traditional church *and* to the new feminist groups. One is a citizen of two cultures, as it were, alternating between the Altar Society and the NOW meeting. This position is inherently unstable; sooner or later jet lag takes its toll. But a number of women choose to endure the tension because they see value in the traditional religious institution even while they experience a fuller sense of truth and liberation in alternative feminist groups. Many may find little or no nourishment themselves in the traditional Sunday worship service, but they continue to attend with their families because they see nothing else in place to help their children. Such women may repair elsewhere to meet their own religious needs, or they may simply let these needs suffer neglect.

Type 5: Women Transforming Church

Women following this fifth model consciously claim both feminism *and* Christianity, and they identify with the prophetic strain that has throughout history criticized injustice in the religious community. Instead of remaining superior and separate, or else existing on a parallel track vis-a-vis the ambiguous institutional church, these women see themselves as working to bring about a more just order within the church at large. Rosemary Radford Ruether is the leading spokeswoman for this type of response, and a full articulation of her liberationist ecclesiology has been published in a 1986 volume called *Women-Church*.[15]

Many who opt for this transformationist model have named themselves as church, perhaps most notably in the two national "women-church" conferences, held in Chicago in 1984 and Cincinnati in 1987. Whether on a large or a small scale, these women gather as church to celebrate their faith, to support each other in the struggle against patriarchy, and to plan ways of remedying injustice in the wider church as well as in society at large.

This fifth model is the one I find most adequate, for it does better justice to the reality of Christianity's ambiguous heritage, which has always combined aspects of liberation *and* oppression, than do either of the extreme models, those of agreement and opposition. Furthermore, the transformationist model seems to offer over the long term a more realistic and a more responsible answer to the current dilemma than does the retreat to separatism, although in some cases a strategic withdrawal may be called for. In general, however, the "women above the church" model tends to lack a principle of self-criticism and to neglect the complex historical and social nature of women's reality, which always includes relationships with men and with the next generation. Likewise the transformationist model is generally preferable to the balancing act of the paradox model, which takes a high psychological toll and also neglects the task of making the Christian religious institution accountable to its best ideals.

Ruether on the Women-Church Movement

It is this growing phenomenon of women's intentional communities of faith and worship that Ruether deals with in her book *Women-Church*. Such communities are springing up, she notes, because Christian feminist women "cannot wait for the institutional churches to reform themselves enough to provide the vehicle of faith and worship that women need in this time." The needs are simply too great to neglect. As Ruether puts it,

> Women in contemporary churches are suffering from linguistic deprivation and eucharistic famine. They can no longer nurture their souls in alienating words which ignore or systematically deny their existence. They are starved for words of life, for symbolic forms which fully and wholeheartedly affirm their personhood and which speak truth about the evils of sexism and the possibilities of a future beyond patriarchy. They desperately need primary communities which nurture their journey into wholeness. . .[16]

Instead of waiting indefinitely, these women are taking responsibility for meeting their own religious needs.

Linking this development with the biblical heritage, Ruether describes the contemporary women-church movement as an "exodus" from patriarchy. She argues that historically "the church" is best understood as a "dialectical interaction" between two elements, namely the "historical institution" and the "spirit-filled community." Her analysis lines up well with that of the Old Testament scholar Walter Brueggemann, who understands the history of the tradition as a constant tension between "royal consciousness" on the one hand, and "prophetic consciousness" on the other.[17] Combining the ideas of Ruether and Brueggemann, one might say that Spirit-filled feminist communities are today involved in the sacred task of keeping prophetic consciousness in dialectical tension with the patriarchal, or royal consciousness, now dominating the historical institution. From a Catholic perspective, however, it is particularly important to recognize the presence of the Spirit in the larger historical institution and not to mistakenly assume that all truth and goodness reside with self-proclaimed feminists, much less that the latter are immune from error and sinfulness. As is the case with the typology of responses, so also the dialectic of Spirit-filled communities and historical institution is an abstraction that has heuristic value but cannot do full justice to the mystery that is the church.

Ruether is aware that the women-church movement may seem separatist and indeed that some participate in it on such a basis, but she argues strongly against any permanent separation from the tradition and opposes the idea of women-church as an end in itself. Rather, women-church represents a necessary stage on a journey toward a "co-human Church," a community of Christian women and men together engaged in "liberation from patriarchy." She is enough of a realist, however, to know that such widely shared conversion from patriarchy is a long way off. She explains:

> Patriarchy is too old and too deeply rooted both in our psyches
> and in our culture and collective life to be quickly analyzed,
> rejected and then overcome in new unity of men and women.
> We must think of Women-Church as a feminist counter-culture
> to the *ecclesia* of patriarchy that must continue for the foresee-
> able future as an exodus both within and on the edges of exist-
> ing church institutions.

"Women-Church means neither leaving the church as a sectarian group," Ruether adds, "nor continuing to fit into it on its terms."[18] In terms of the typology, she objects to the "Women Above the Church" model as well as to the "Women and Church in Paradox" model, for these options function to cut off the interaction needed for the eventual transformation of the historical institution. Other thinkers besides Ruether have also articulated a transformationist ideal, and with them I am persuaded that of the several types of responses, this represents the best ethical ideal for women in relation to patriarchal Christianity.[19] In certain circumstances, however, another response may be more appropriate for some women; this is something women must discern for themselves.

In sum, then, the answer to the question of how women are responding to the institutional voices of patriarchy is that all five responses are being made today: there are women content with the church, and women utterly opposed to it; there are women who opt for a sectarian solution somewhere "above" the church, and women who paradoxically maintain church membership *on the institution's terms* while at the same time claiming feminist values; and finally, there are women dedicated to transforming the church into a community liberated from patriarchy. On the normative level I have claimed that the fifth is generally the most adequate response and to conclude I shall sketch what a transformationist response ought to involve.

In the first place, Christian women should strive to be as consistently transformationist as possible. This stance will mean building women-church into an exodus movement that flourishes in dialectical, transformative tension with the larger church. "Exodus" is not meant here as withdrawing from the institution, but rather as going out from the injustices of the present toward the possibilities of the future. This movement beckons the entire Christian community to be more faithful to gospel ideals of justice and mutuality in its own structures and relationships. In this process, women must organize to provide sustenance for our Christian lives, to integrate our feminism with our experiences of the sacred, and to challenge and support one another in the struggle for liberation. We must protect ourselves and others from patriarchal rituals that function as "occasions" of the sins of anger and despair and provide in their stead liturgies that are occasions of hope and sources of strength for the journey. We must not retreat permanently to sectarian isolation and complacency nor be governed by patriarchal definitions of what church membership requires. We must rather claim the Christian tradition as our own and take responsibility for shaping its future.

And what of the brethren? Christian men should share the egalitarian feminist vision. They should support and encourage transformationist women and they should design creative ways to facilitate their own liberation from patriarchy. As Ruether puts it, our brothers should join us in the exodus. This will entail respecting our need for female caucuses within the broader feminist community, and also establishing their own male feminist caucuses in which to sort out and celebrate their liberation.

And finally, transformationist women and men should be self-critical. The transformationist ideal is not easily fulfilled, and there is always the risk of slipping into one of the other responses for less than adequate reasons. In fact, the five types are more than categories for analyzing how women in general are responding; the typology is also a good tool for scrutinizing one's own inner conflicts and inconsistencies. The shades of thoughtless accommodation, indiscriminate rejection, romantic sectarianism, and pusillanimous biculturalism lurk in all our psyches. The "Woman Content with the Church" surfaces when we repress our anger against oppression or fail to see the injustice in our communities, even the ones we name "women-church"; the "Woman Against the Church" emerges when we indulge that anger indiscriminately or fail to seek constructive alternatives to what we are critiquing. The "Woman Above the Church" appears when we yield to complacency and let the supportive community of co-feminists become the only group that matters. And the "Woman and Church in Paradox" is evident in all our failures—whether from timidity, laziness, or plain muddleheadedness—to make the church of Christ the sign of hope to the nations that our just and compassionate God intends it to be.

There is reason, obviously, for even the most committed Christian feminists, women and men alike, to repent and seek forgiveness for our sins and inadequacies. But in view of what we know of God—whose mercy is above all her works and who is present with us both to will and to accomplish—there is even more reason to celebrate the liberation from personal as well as from social sin.

My next point may already be obvious to many, but in view of the situation in certain Christian communions—Missouri Synod Lutheran and Roman Catholic, for example—it is still necessary to belabor the obvious. Given the fact of this liberation already in progress and coming in its fullness, it is truly meet and just, right and salutary, therefore and above all, for women-church to give thanks—yes, to celebrate Eucharist—and to do this in the name and memory of Jesus, whose ethical ideals, as his followers insisted from the beginning, included the belief that if it came to a choice, one should obey God and not men. I have heard something to that effect attributed to Peter himself in Acts 5, where Luke describes a controversy between early Christian apostles and first-century Jewish leaders. This text has bearing on the present controversy between Christians with

the new moral vision of equality and certain contemporary church officials. Much has changed, but then as now, the issue involves *authority:*

> So they brought them [the apostles] and stood them before the
> Council; and the High Priest began his examination. "We ex-
> pressly ordered you," he said, "to desist from teaching in that
> name; and what has happened? You have filled Jerusalem
> with your teaching, and you are trying to make us responsible
> for that man's death." Peter replied for himself and the
> apostles: "We must obey God rather than men." (Acts 5:27-
> 29)

Today feminist women and men alike are hearing from the high priests
of patriarchy, "We do not approve of your teaching." This is said at times
with force—not the literal sword that threatened Peter and his companions,
but certainly with the bureaucratic sword. And in Acts 5:38-39 we are told
of a Jewish thinker whose wisdom stopped the sword on that occasion.
What Gamaliel said to the high priest then remains instructive today:

> "[L]eave them alone. For if this idea of theirs or its execution
> is of human origin, it will collapse; but if it is from God, you
> will never be able to put them down, and you risk finding
> yourselves at war with God."

Gamaliel's words did not prevent the flogging and the orders to stop
speaking in Jesus' name. But neither did these measures prevent the
gospel from being preached.

Notes

1. This is discussed more fully in Anne E. Patrick, "Character and Community: Curran and a Church Coming of Age," in William W. May, ed., *Vatican Authority and American Catholic Dissent* (New York: Crossroad, 1987), pp. 127-143.

2. For an example of a work that does examine the ethics of church practice critically in the light of faith, see Leonardo Boff, *Church: Charism and Power* (New York: Crossroad, 1985).

3. See James M. Gustafson, *Can Ethics Be Christian?* (Chicago: University of Chicago Press, 1975), p. 179.

4. Matthew Arnold, *God and the Bible* (Boston: James R. Osgood and Company, 1876), p. xiii.

5. "New Patterns of Relationship: Beginnings of a Moral Revolution," in Walter Burghardt, ed., *Woman: New Dimensions* (New York: Paulist Press, 1977), p. 52.

6. For an historical discussion of this topic, see Gerda Lerner, *The Creation of Patriarchy* (New York: Oxford University Press, 1986). In general, patriarchy may be understood as a social or structural manifestation of the attitude of sexist discrimination against women. For an ethical analysis of "sexism," see Patricia Beattie Jung, "Give Her Justice," *America* 150 (April 14, 1984):276-78. With Jung, I understand the terms "sexism" and "feminism" as dialectically related. I employ "feminist" here in a broad sense to indicate a position that involves (1) a solid conviction of the equality of women and men, and (2) a commitment to reform society, including religious society, so that the full equality of women is respected, which requires also reforming the thought systems that legitimate the present unjust social order. Both women and men can thus be "feminist," and within this broad category there is enormous variety in levels of commitment, degrees of explicitness of commitment, and, of course, opinions regarding specific problems and their solutions.

7. Quoted from Eric Marshall and Stuart Hemple, "Children's Letters to God," in Casey Miller and Kate Swift, *Words and Women: New Language in New Times* (Garden City, NY: Anchor Books, 1977), p. 70.

8. Unfortunately the first draft of the U.S. bishops' pastoral letter on women's concerns, "Partners in the Mystery of Redemption," [*Origins* 17 (April 21, 1988): 757-788] ignores the reality of internalized oppression, even while recognizing that sexism is sinful.

9. H. Richard Niebuhr, *Christ and Culture* (New York: Harper and Row, 1951), p. 10.

10. Ibid., p. 44.

11. Jackson W. Carroll, Barbara Hargrove, and Adair T. Lummis, *Women of the Cloth: A New Opportunity for the Churches* (New York: Harper and Row, 1983); Andrew M. Greeley and Mary G. Durkin, *Angry Catholic Women* (Chicago: Thomas More Press, 1984). Greeley makes the following observation in the sociological analysis section of *Angry Catholic Women*: "Obviously it would be desirable to study the situation of women in the Catholic Church from the point of view of a research project which was designed specifically with that goal in mind and which asked a variety of questions to be dictated by such an interest. However, until such a project is funded (and don't anyone hold their breath!) secondary

analysis is a useful and valid though somewhat limited technique for understanding the problems of women in the Roman Catholic Church" (p.12).

12. Although the "Voices of Affirmation" quoted in the 1988 draft of the U.S. bishops' pastoral letter on "women's concerns" are by no means limited to this first type, they are heavily representative of it. The method employed in this draft, which involves accepting conflicting analyses of certain problems without making judgments on their relative merits, is a flawed one and quite a departure from the more coherent normative approach taken in the earlier pastoral letters on peace and the economy. I discuss this more fully in a response to the 1988 draft published in *Commonweal* (June 3, 1988), pp. 365-66.

13. See Chapter Five, "The Bonds of Freedom: Sisterhood as Antichurch," in Mary Daly, *Beyond God the Father: Toward a Philosophy of Women's Liberation* (Boston: Beacon, 1973).

14. Greeley and Durkin, pp. 41-42, 49.

15. Rosemary Radford Ruether, *Women-Church: Theology and Practice of Feminist Liturgical Communities* (San Francisco: Harper & Row, 1986).

16. *Ibid.,* pp. 4-5.

17. See Walter Brueggemann, *The Prophetic Imagination* (Philadelphia: Fortress Press, 1978).

18. Ruether, p. 62.

19. For examples of other Catholic and Protestant scholars who stress the transformationist ideal, see Anne E. Carr, *Transforming Grace: Christian Tradition and Women's Experience* (San Francisco: Harper & Row, 1988); Beverly Wildung Harrison, "Keeping Faith in a Sexist Church: Not for Women Only," in her book *Making the Connections: Essays in Feminist Social Ethics,* edited by Carol S. Robb (Boston: Beacon, 1985), pp. 206-34; Maria Riley, "Women, Church and Patriarchy," *America* (May 5, 1984):333-38; and, Mary Jo Weaver, *New Catholic Women: A Challenge to Traditional Religious Authority* (New York: Harper and Row, 1985).

3

Freedom, Responsibility, Authority

David Tracy
University of Chicago

Philosophical Reflections: Theology in the Academic Context

At every moment of theology's task, a principal social context of the theologian will be the academy. However, theologians are usually participating members of a particular church tradition as well and also attempt to be responsible citizens of a particular society. Theology is peculiar as a discipline because it attempts to speak to and from three contexts: the context of the academy, the context of the church, and the context of the wider society. In those capacities, theologians present the results of their academic findings as proposals relevant to either church or society or both.

If this is an accurate reading of the basic academic task of theology and of the different contexts to which theologians may address their findings as proposals for critical consideration, then it follows that it is impossible to discuss the theologian's freedom and responsibility to authority without clarifying how authority functions in each context (academy, church and society) and what distinct freedoms and responsibilities are available to the theologian in each context. Criteria for authority, responsibility, and freedom are context-dependent. Criteria in the academy (which, to repeat, is a primary locus of theology *as theology*) are not necessarily transferrable without revision into criteria for authority, responsibility, and freedom in a particular church, with a particular church order, or into a particular society, with a particular constitution.

The first task for the theologian, therefore, is to clarify these concepts (freedom, responsibility and authority) in relationship to the social context of theology, the academy. There the situation in principle, if not always in fact, is clear. Any university which honors academic freedom insists that such freedom must respect canons of authority appropriate to the academy. In the academy, the only relevant authority is professional competence. The authority of any theologian's work in the academy is the same as that of any other scholar, no more, no less; it is the authority of an expertise established by persuasive argument and disciplined inquiry. The *de facto* authorities to whom theologians address their proposals are fellow professionals who can judge these interpretations of religious traditions and the contemporary situation or any claims they make for meaning and truth.

The responsibility of the theologian in the academy is simply the expression of this freedom: that is, never to allow oneself to express unexamined private opinions as public proposals. Rather every theologian must insist upon common canons of inquiry for theological studies. Those canons will not, in principle, be different from the canons of inquiry for religious studies save that the scholar in religious studies *may* raise explicitly the question of the truth of the religion under study, whereas the theologian *must* raise this question explicitly and address it.

However, the theologian may also be a believing member of a church tradition as well as a responsible citizen of a particular society. The question recurs, therefore: what is the meaning of freedom and responsibility when theologians address their proposals to either church or society? Theologians address their proposals to both society and church. This is especially true, of course, of theologians involved in theological social ethics, or feminist theologies, or in political or liberation theologies. In principle, there is no difference between the freedom and responsibilities entailed by addressing theological proposals to the wider society and the same freedom and responsibility any scholar in any discipline has in addressing her/his proposals to society. Consider for example political theory. When political theorists in the American academic setting, such as John Rawls, Noam Chomsky, or Robert Nisbet (to cite three very different proposals) present their scholarly results as proposals—not only as political theorists but for society—they too depend on two factors: first, the authority (as persuasive argument) of their academic work; second, the need to translate that work into a proposal (for example, for social justice) for a particular society. As soon as scholars make the second move as well, they must also take account of the *de jure* and *de facto* authorities of that particular society. We have a constitution; we have laws. If you are going to argue for civil disobedience, for example, as Thoreau argued, and as Martin Luther King, Jr., as a theologian and as a political theorist, argued, you can either make it as a purely academic argument or, as King did, as an argument that it is proper, in certain circumstances, to practice civil disobedience in American society. In short, they must now argue their case anew in relationship not only to the canons of inquiry in the academy but in terms of the canons of *de jure* and *de facto* authority in this particular society.

This analogy of the political theorist in society, I hope, is helpful. For there is no real difference, in principle, of a political theorist making proposals to American society or a theologian making proposals to either society or church or both. What both situations alert us to is that the crucial notions 'authority', 'responsibility', and 'freedom' appropriate to the academy are unlikely to be synonymous with those same concepts as now translated for a particular society or a particular church which has particular *de jure* and *de facto* authorities. Once those factors are seriously considered, the context-dependent nature of the theologian's 'freedom' and 'responsibility' in relationship to ecclesial or societal authorities can also be clarified.

Although the societal focus is both illuminating and important, the focus of our discussion today is more on the responsibility and freedom of the theologian in relationship to the church rather than to society. I shall spend the remainder of my time, therefore, on the relationship to the church. This is not to deny, of course, the public character of theological proposals and their relevance for society. For instance, the American bishop's pastorals have strength precisely because they try to make their arguments on inner-Christian, indeed, inner-Catholic grounds *and* they try to make an argument for the wider society on grounds that in principle that wider society could accept. Any theologian who is also a believing member of a particular church community is likely to view her/his theology as relevant to that community, and not just to fellow theologians in the academy. As such, theologians rethink their theological research in reference to the issues of the church community—even non-ecclesiologists like myself.

In the academy, therefore, theological research as theological must be accorded the same freedom and responsibilities as any other research: the authority of theologians is synonymous with their ability to provide persuasive arguments and their fidelity to the canons of inquiry for the discipline. But when that same theologian presents the results of that theological inquiry as a proposal for church or society, a further responsibility is entailed. That responsibility is the need to see how the proposal relates to the *de jure* and *de facto* authorities of that community. I understand *de jure* authority to mean (in the correct definition of Stanley Benn) "a rule-created competence" whereby the competence (for example, to command obedience) is itself derived from rules and must, therefore, be limited and restrained by rules. *De facto* authority ordinarily arises from *de jure* authority—as judges are responsible to the constitution--and exists whenever one person recognizes another as entitled to command in certain situations. Both *de jure* and *de facto* authority are rule-governed. Both are distinct from the phenomenon with which they are often confused, namely, coercive *power* wherein there is no limit or rule.

I assume that in the Christian tradition there is a commonly acknowledged *de jure* authority (minimally, for all Christians, the canonical scriptural texts) as well as distinct *de jure* and *de facto* authorities established in specific church-orders. What is theologically relevant to note about this crucial distinction is this: all *de facto* ecclesial authorities are not only distinct from coercive power but, precisely as authorities, must also be limited by those rules empowering their *de facto* authority. This limitation on authority means that if a theological proposal for the church community disagrees with the present theological position of the acknowledged *de facto* authorities, the theologian can still in principle appeal to the *de jure* authority (of scripture, for instance, or the authoritative apostolic witness or the great tradition) to make their responsible case, including the notion of responsible dissent.

This principle, let us note, must logically be acknowledged by any *de facto* ecclesial authority which is not merely disguised coercive power but real authority—that is, acknowledged competence to command in certain situations grounded in the limits and restraints imposed by the *de jure* authorities recognized by the entire church community.

In the Christian community, most Christian churches, whatever the particular character of their *de facto* authorities (bishops, synods, congregational polity, pope, council, presbytery, etc.) acknowledge at least the canonical scriptures as a necessary even if not sufficient *de jure* authority. Hence any appeal by theologians to that *de jure* authority for their proposals (e.g., appeals to a 'canon within the canon') are entirely responsible actions. Such responsible dissent even from *de facto* authorities is entirely appropriate to the freedom of any member of the church community. In fact, I believe one can properly argue that even on the *de jure* authority of the scriptures, other *de jure* authorities are acknowledged by the Christian church, certainly by the Catholic Church: viz. reason, contemporary experience, and living tradition.

Yet important (and controversial) as these theological conclusions may be, from my own understanding of what constitutes a responsible proposal for my own Catholic church community, those conclusions are not presently necessary to make my principal point: namely, that any *de facto* authority which really is authority and not disguised coercive power is necessarily grounded in *de jure* authority. Thus it is terribly important to clarify what those relationships are. One of the issues would be episcopacy and primacy, but only one within that larger context. I repeat that the most helpful analogy is precisely the analogy of civil disobedience. When is civil disobedience a responsible act? It is a responsible act when the person involved in civil disobedience tries to make a case, not just as an academic thinking about civil disobedience, but in relationship to the authorities of the society to whom one is being disobedient, and to a *particular* law. The person argues that the basic *de jure* authorities demand this disobedience. Likewise, any theologian may appeal to that *de jure* authority to challenge present or past decisions of *de facto* authorities. Any theological challenge argued on the basis of the *de jure* authority is, in principle, a responsible challenge and should be so acknowledged as an in-principled possibility by *de facto* authorities, however much they may dislike the proposal itself.

I recognize, of course, that these distinctions set only very general conditions for reflection on responsible free actions of theologians in any church community. They cannot resolve the necessary arguments in those communities on specific proposals. But these distinctions challenge the frequent—and confusing—notion that authority is really synonymous with coercive power. They also challenge equally the familiar notion that the nature of freedom, responsibility, and authority need not be seen in context, but are concepts that are the *same* in academy, society, and church. Rather, as I have argued, those notions receive their exact meaning only from their context. They are necessarily context-dependent. The persuasive authority of professional competence of the scholar in the academy is related to, but not identical with, the acceptance of the rule-delimited *de jure* authority of particular churches or particular societies.

The theologians primary responsibility *as a theologian,* as academic, is to the canons of inquiry grounding professional competence in theology. Any authority (as persuasive) the theologian may personally possess comes from the acknowledgement by competent professional experts, or readers, of the persuasive power of her or his argument and from her or his fidelity to the canons of inquiry in the discipline. If I may make a reference to Dr. Scanlon's discussion of Gadamer's notion of authority: certain texts or certain arguments are *persuasive* and in that sense authoritative, as distinct from commanding obedience. That is to say, it's an appeal to the persuasive power of the argument in the academy. I think Gadamer is exactly right on that, but then when you move into society—as Plato saw—with laws, law always have some coercive element. Then one has to reflect further on authority, which is not only the authority of the authoritative classic, or the authoritative argument of the scholar. When theologians also make proposals to church or society, they do so as free and responsible members of that church or society. They must then make their case for that community in a responsible way: that is, in terms of an argument of the *de jure* authorities of that community. If they disagree on particular issues with the *de facto* authorities of society, they can responsibly appeal to the *de jure* authorities to make their case.

What seems to be occurring in the present neo-conservative resurgence cutting across all the churches, indeed cutting across the culture as a whole, is a vast confusion of the notions of authority and power. For the conservative instinct on authority, for example, of a classic conservative like Edmund Burke, is not that authority is simply power (that is a reactionary instinct), but that authority is important for any community and should be used or it will be lost. The contemporary neo-conservative may either share that belief or, in a fury at the twilight of authority (in Robert Nisbet's famous phrase), effectively confuse authority with coercive power.

The authentic liberal impulse on authority—the instinct of Locke and later 'consent theorists', and certainly of American democracy—is that authority is justifiable in certain circumstances, but, if abused, will be lost. The widespread concern with authority across the Christian churches and the culture as a whole provides some persuasive evidence that this liberal instinct for distinguishing authority and power, while still justifying authority as rule-created competence, should not be lost.

Where the liberal and the conservative divide is in their analysis of the heart of the problem of authority. But they need not divide on the distinct meanings of authority, freedom, and responsibility in academy, society, and church. If theologians could agree on these general rubrics for the context-dependent meanings of responsibility, authority and freedom of theologians in academy, church and society, we might find again that there was a theological conversation, not a power-struggle. For conversation by definition is rule governed and only persuades; it does not coerce.

Theological Reflections:
The Catholic Construal of Church

The more properly theological context for church (and, therefore, authority in church) may be clarified, I suggest, by reflection on that reality in Newman, von Hugel and Murray. I choose them because I agree with them and believe they represent—together—some of the best reflections we have on this complex issue.

This Catholic insistence on both unity and diversity finds ample articulation in the reflections of Newman. His reflections show with great subtlety how there must be many 'ways,' for there are so many kinds of individuals in such different cultures and classes, with such different temperaments and with such different levels of intellectual, moral and religious development. At the same time, for the Catholic, these many ways are grounded in and spiritually responsible to the one way of God's revelation in the Word as mediated to us in the great tradition of scripture, doctrine, symbol, and sacrament. This Catholic sense for spiritual diversity amidst spiritual unity finds further expression in Newman's reflections on these central objective realities of all Catholic spirituality: a sense of tradition, a sense of the wider community, a firm affirmation of doctrine as objective, a sacramental envisionment of all reality. These fundamental Catholic affirmations, moreover, led Newman to insist that the modern emphasis on 'personal experience' could be fully at home in Catholic spirituality. For doctrine, community, tradition, and sacrament are the sure ground of all Catholic spiritual experience. As such, they do not impoverish but enrich the personal religious experience of every Catholic by providing the common ground which helps the believer on the great dilemmas of a spiritual life: the meanings of conscience, the vagaries of emotion and feeling, and above all, the gradual accumulation over a lifetime of probabilities into firm certitude. The believer can develop a spiritual certitude certain that the way is founded in objective-as-revealed truth. English devotional practices, Newman insists, are unlikely to be the same as Italian religious practices. They are no less Catholic. Both are firmly grounded in doctrine, sacrament, tradition and community.

Newman's reflections on the church bear a distinctly Catholic mark. When Newman appealed to the 'idea' of the Church, he meant idea, not as an abstraction, but as one's deepest sense of the concrete whole and its constituent parts. 'Idea', for him, meant not an abstraction from reality, as it usually now means, but the reality itself, the reality of church, as spiritually sensed but never fully understood. I think that *is* the Catholic sense. As Augustine sometimes said, "If you ask me what time is, I can't tell you, if you don't ask me, then I know." Christianity itself in his *Essay on the Development of Doctrine* was such an organic idea: a reality that is sensed, felt, understood, and yielding itself to partial, incomplete, but true understanding as it developed through the centuries. The Church, as an idea, *is* the objective reality. Church *is* the Body of Christ. Church is constituted by the Spirit of Christ. That is why only the truly spiritual can understand the church, and why the Christian experiences and understands Christ and the Spirit in and through the church. That is why the church is so important to the Catholic; that's why the conflicts are so intense, because it is so important.

The idea of the church was never for Newman a mere idea but the polity which is the church existing here and now: the gifted reality as well as infuriating human faults and continuing need for self-reform. Catholic spirituality senses and understands the Church in its unity and in its distinct parts—parts which can never efface the antecedent divinely graced unity. Catholic spirituality also struggles to discern what part of the church needs strengthening, or development, or correction of excesses by reform.

Newman described three offices of the church: the prophetical, or teaching office, the ruling office, and the office of ministry. He described as well the temptations of each of these. The temptation of the prophetical teaching office (theology) is rationalism; that of the ruling office is coercive power; that of the sacred ministry and piety is superstition. Each temptation has been yielded to in the history of the church; each temptation always needs to be spotted in particular situations, and healed, if possible. The temptation, moreover, of each part is to think itself the whole church. Thus could Newman appeal to history when, in the fourth century, most of the bishops abandoned the true christological doctrine in the Arian controversy and the church for its very life in that period depended not on the bishops but on the laity to maintain its true identity. This example impelled Newman to insist on the need to consult the laity and to defend the notion of the 'sensus fidelium' as a truly ecclesial sense. This insistence gave him great difficulties with some in the Vatican.

In sum, one finds in Newman a clearly Catholic sense where the realities of doctrine, sacrament, tradition, community, and above all church as Body of Christ comprised of three equally indispensable functions form the spirituality of all individuals and cultures—you cannot eliminate any one of them, and you cannot allow one of them to take over. This formation takes place in such a manner that there is a great diversity of spiritual ways but also a common mind on the central reality of the Spirit's Indwelling presence to the individual soul in communion with the Church as the mediation of that Spiritual Presence of Christ.

Newman's exceptional sensitivity on the need for great diversity and great powers of critical discernment in the ever-shifting historical and theological reality of the Church made his spirituality influential for many modern Catholics. His spiritual sense was both unmistakably Catholic in its sense of church, and clearly modern in the need for ever-present criticism. This sense pervades the rootedness in Catholic tradition and the openness to other religious traditions and to modernity in the major decrees of the Second Vatican Council. Post-conciliar Catholic spiritualities, at their best, are informed by this same inclusive and objective Newmanian spirit.

One major example of the influence of Newman on his younger contemporaries may be found in the thought of Baron Frederick von Hugel. Von Hugel expands Newman's basic paradigm of these three offices: the teaching, the ruling, and the ministerial. He then tried to think of *any* religion by using Newman's notion of the three offices. What are the three elements, he asked, that must interact in any living religion?

Although perhaps best remembered for his complex role in the 'Modernist crisis' of the early twentieth century, Baron von Hugel's contribution to modern Catholic spirituality may best be witnessed in his classic work *The Mystical Element of Religion as Studied in Saint Catherine of Genoa and her Friends*. Here, as in his other works, one may see the 'modern' side of Catholic spirituality that first erupted in the Modernist crisis.

After its early suppression by church authorities, it returned in more substantive Catholic form in the great reform movements of early twentieth century Catholicism and culminated in the Second Vatican Council. The strengths of the Catholic modernist movement are all present in von Hugel: his insistence on historical consciousness and on historico-critical methods for biblical studies and church history; his development of a philosophy of 'personalism' that highlights the existential character of religious truth; his openness to modern science and indeed to the genuine accomplishments of the modern period; his inner-Christian ecumenical spirit united to his respect for the other great religious traditions.

He defended the use of historico-critical methods by Alfred Loisy and the emphasis on personal experience by George Tyrrell. He resisted, in his writing, in his voluminous correspondence, and his actions, the triumphant style of the then powerful Ultramontane Roman Catholicism. He honored the institutional reality of the Catholic church while insisting on the ever-present danger of over-centralization, clericalism and bureaucratization. And yet, however open to modernity and however critical of the institutional church reality of his day, von Hugel maintained a Catholic sense of the need for a balance and harmony of elements. Precisely his Catholic sense of balance led him to develop a position that, however sympathetic to the historical contributions of Loisy and the brilliant experiential insights of Tyrrell, made his position less like theirs and more like Newman's and Blondel's.

Von Hugel's own work may be viewed as a genuinely modern Catholic development of Newman's insight into Catholic spiritual diversity-in-unity. On the one hand, von Hugel used that Newmanian insight to expand its range not solely on the reality of the church but on the reality of religion itself. On the other hand, von Hugel was far less theological than Newman and less concerned, therefore, with showing the theological reality of the church as the presence of Christ's Indwelling Spirit. His principle concern was to develop a philosophy of religion that could show the actuality of the concrete person as a unity-in-diversity and thereby the actuality of religion itself as having the character of a concrete person with both great multiplicity and real unity.

Philosophically, von Hugel (in harmony with the radical empiricism and personalism of his period) developed a personalist philosophy that argued for the presence of emotional, intellectual and volitional elements acting in harmony in every concrete person. He believed, as did Coleridge and Newman before him, that a prior unity is given to any concrete personal reality. That reality can be sensed and lived but never fully analyzed. One can, however, note the need for the complex development of each person for the full development and harmonization of the emotional, intellectual, and volitional elements.

This personalist model deeply informs von Hugel's discussion of religion in *The Mystical Element of Religion*. For there he attempts to show, through the action-in-the-everyday spirituality of St. Catherine of Genoa, that every living religion bears its clearest analogue in the living person. As with knowing and trusting a person, so the believer knows and trusts the concrete reality of God disclosed in the religion. As with the religion, the living unity and trust is concretely realized before analysis and criticism are forthcoming. As with a person, so too religion is constituted by three principal functions which are analogous to the emotional, intellectual, and volitional elements of the person. As with the person, there is always a need both to develop each element and its interrelationships to the other elements to achieve the balance and harmony of an authentic personality.

In the case of religion, this personalist analogy led von Hugel to his promising suggestion for understanding the three major elements comprising a historical religion. These elements are: (1) the external, authoritative, historical, traditional and institutional (analogous to the volitional element in the person); (2) the critical-historical and synthetic-philosophical (analogous to the intellectual) and (3) the mystical (analogous to the emotional). He takes Newman's three offices for the church and relates them to the development of any individual. Every individual, he says, balances the emotional, intellectual and volitional elements in her or his life for full development, and needs to recognize that each element will try to take over. Likewise, religion needs to balance 1) its historical, authoritative, 2) its critical, philosophical, and 3) its mystical elements.

Von Hugel attempted, above all, to be faithful both to the complexity of Catholic Christianity as a unified religion with several aspects and also its peculiarly modern intellectual needs. He combined the Catholic search for harmony with an openness to modernity. Note the language he uses for each of the elements:

(1) the 'institutional' is to be affirmed but only as related to the necessary fullness of this 'external' element, as authoritative, historical, and traditional.

(2) the 'intellectual' element must include not only the philosophical-synthetic (as in the classic Scholastic Theologies and their less happy—for von Hugel—neo-Scholastic successors) but also the critical-historical (as in biblical and doctrinal studies); and I think most of us would now add, critical-political, liberation, and feminist theologies;

(3) the 'mystical' element is not merely 'passive' but includes action as well. For von Hugel Catholic mystical spiritualities, such as the

spirituality of Catherine of Genoa, are action-oriented and incarnational in principle. My own belief is that the most important movement occurring in theology today is the attempt to develop a "prophetic-mystical" position. In Latin American theology and feminist theology and political theology, that is the heart of the matter. If you can show how both the prophetic and the mystical are alive at one and the same time you are really aiding the situation. The analogue in Chinese culture is an extraordinary attempt to relate the more mystical Taoist and Buddhist traditions with the more civil-order, justice-oriented, classical Confucian traditions. I would say that in Catholic, Protestant and Jewish theology what is happening across the board are these attempts to develop a prophetic-mystical position.

What Newman attempted to show under the theological rubric of church, von Hugel addressed under the philosophical rubric of 'religion'. Both can be considered classic modern Catholic sensibilities. Both unite an insistence that the concrete reality of God is mediated in the concrete historical form of church (Newman) and religion (von Hugel). Both insisted that only attention to that concreteness as sensed by the believer could assure both the personalism and the objectivity true to Catholic spirituality. Both felt no need to disallow this unity amidst great spiritual diversity: a diversity occasioned by different temperaments, cultures and historical periods and a diversity grounded in the triple office of the church (Newman) or the threefold elements of concrete religion (von Hugel). Both insisted that true Catholic discernment is grounded in this sense of God's reality as mediated to us in Jesus Christ and the church. Both also insisted on the constant spiritual need for Catholics to discern the needed corrections and developments of these three functions as well to discern the contributions of modernity for Catholic self-understanding. Both Newman and von Hugel (like Maurice Blondel in France and J.A. Moehler in Germany) developed influential spiritualities because they were both Catholic and modern.

In the American discussion on freedom, responsibility and authority, the primary figure is John Courtney Murray. In his final years, Murray began to rethink his ecclesiology along Vatican II lines from the analogical perspective of the public realm as always demanding argument, persuasion, and reason. Although Murray's reflections in this direction never reached final form, his new envisionment of the church deserves more notice than it has received. Once again, Murray's major category is dialogue and the freedom that dialogue necessarily entails. What analogical possibilities for the church does the notion of a public realm for the body politic suggest?

Such analogies as may exist can only be clarified, of course, by noting both the similarities and differences between the political order and the church. Murray was firmly theological in his insistence on those differences: the two societies differ in origin and end and could possess therefore, only analogical, not univocal, public orders. Murray had previously analyzed these differences between church and secular society in terms of Bellarmine's famous distinction of two 'societies'. However, he quickly saw that Vatican II had released new theological possibilities. By translating the image of 'The People of God' into the clearer designation 'the Christian community', Murray began to see a way forward to incorporate dialogue and freedom more explicitly into church order. The next step would have been for Murray to ask what structural changes are needed as a way to adjudicate the inevitable controversies of the Christian community.

The theological meaning of the church, for Murray, is a divinely graced community. It is a communion having the common functions of witness and service. On this 'community' model, the church is also, but only secondarily, a society with a juridical order and structures of authority. Just as secular governments are meant to serve the interests and needs of the public realm, and not to replace them, so too the juridical and *de facto* authority structures of the church are meant to serve the needs for the unity and order of the common meanings, and the common need for witness and service in the Christian community. That was also both von Hugel's and Newman's criticism of the Ultramontanism of their day. The situation is like that of political theorists who argue against identifying state and society; if you ever allow the state to become, in effect, the whole notion of society then there *is* no more public realm that is worth mentioning. There is then no realm where true dialogue and freedom can occur. Just as the grounding reality of the body politic is the realm of public reasoning on common meanings, empowered by dialogue and freedom, so too the grounding reality of the church is the realm of graced communion in common meanings. Love empowers this realm. Within the church, dialogue and freedom are encouraged so that controversy is not ended prematurely by coercion but channelled into living persuasion. Notice how love, dialogue and freedom are not sentimental concepts here, but are concrete concepts for rethinking the church order.

For Murray, love, dialogue, and freedom defined his emerging notion of the church as the 'Christian community'. This is a promising if still unfinished vision for a new church order. Such a notion would have clear structural implications. Though the earlier 'perfect society' model for church life had clear disadvantages, it had the intellectual advantage of relating a theological vision of church (an ecclesiology) to a social reality (a social and political theory). Murray's developing model of community has similar advantages. Since the church is a divinely graced communion of persons united in a common meaning, then *caritas* must ground this community, just as analogously justice informs a political community. Love, even more than justice, demands dialogue; dialogue, in turn, demands genuine freedom. This is not, of course, to deny in any way the need to relate love to justice in any church order. The point is that, theologically construed, love as *caritas* transforms, but can never replace justice, in the true Catholic view. Love without justice is always in danger of becoming sentimental. Justice without love is always in danger of becoming self-righteous.

Though the notions of justice in the political realm can inform us, they too have to be informed even more radically by the more demanding power of Christian love, and then relate that to justice. Such a theological-social vision informs any ecclesiology desiring to be faithful to both the demands of a theological understanding of the church and to the need to actualize that vision in concrete social forms for the Christian community. Juridical orders and structures of authority must be rethought in the context of this new theological vision. One can only regret that Murray never lived to complete this inchoate but promising theological envisionment of the new church order demanded by the Vatican II understanding of church. One can only hope that the dialogue—in freedom and love—on how to constitute that order will continue. John Courtney Murray's controversies with the authorities of both church and state freed him to rethink the principles of what constitutes genuine controversy in any genuine community. Those principles remain. Murray's whole life and work exemplified these: the need for argument, for dialogue, for freedom, and for love. On these principles, as in many other central issues, John Courtney Murray and Archbishop Hunthausen stand together.

4

The Doctrinal Limits to Papal Teaching Authority

Peter Chirico, S.S.
Institute for Theological Studies
Seattle University

Introduction

Official teaching on the papacy concentrates upon the comprehensiveness of its governing and teaching authority. That official teaching has made clear that the pope possesses (a) an infallible teaching authority whose exercise leads to doctrines that are irreformable without the consent of the Church, and (b) an ultimate governing authority which is supreme, universal, immediate, and ordinary. Practically nothing in the official teaching deals extensively with the obligations of the papacy and the limits of its powers.[1]

This official forgetfulness of limits in papal authority has led to malaise around any ecumenical venture with other churches.[2] However, Catholic theologians have made efforts to remedy the situation since the Second Vatican council. For example, in a perceptive article, Karl Rahner indicated a number of often unnoticed limits and obligations binding the pope in the exercise of his office.[3] More recently Patrick Granfield has summarized much of the theological discussion on the restrictions binding the papal office.[4]

In this paper I shall concentrate on the doctrinal limits to *papal teaching authority.* This means that I shall not discuss papal primacy or governing authority at all; I did so in an address given at Graymoor in November, 1987, and soon to be published.[5] Further, I shall discuss only *doctrinal limitations,* that is, limitations which flow from the very nature of the papal office and which necessarily bind the pope. Hence, I shall not deal with possible legal limits to papal authority or with the voluntary renunciation of authority by a pope. I believe that legal and voluntary limitations of authority are ultimately ineffectual because they can be overthrown by a future pope.[6]

Much of this paper is speculative and unitive. I attempt to draw conclusions about limitations on papal authority which are not usually drawn. I believe that these conclusions are valid because they flow from the linkage of known aspects of the tradition which up to now have not been linked. Whether my conclusions are valid or not will have to be left to the give and take that has long accompanied reflections of this type in the Church.

The paper is divided into two parts. The first treats the limitations involved in the exercise of the pope's infallible magisterium (teaching power). The second treats his non-infallible or merely authentic teaching authority.

The Pope's Infallible Teaching Authority

The Teaching of Vatican I

The First Vatican Council officially proclaimed the dogma of papal infallibility. That dogma possesses three aspects: the relationship of papal infallibility to the infallibility of the Church; the conditions under which papal infallibility is exercised; the results of the exercise of that infallibility.[7]

First, *primary infallibility rests in the whole Church.* The pope has no infallibility independent of the Church. In fact, in the exercise of his infallible magisterium the pope can only express the infallibility of the whole Church.

Second, there are very clear conditions for the exercise of papal infallibility:

a) The pope must be proclaiming a *revealed truth,* a doctrine of faith or morals;

b) He must be exercising his *supreme apostolic authority;*

c) He must intend to *proclaim* such a doctrine *definitively;*

d) He must be intending to *bind all* the faithful.

Third, when the conditions above are exercised by the pope, he truly expresses the infallible grasp of teaching resident in the Church and his pronouncements are *"irreformable,"* even without the prior or subsequent consent of the Church.

Assumptions Often Made

This brief restatement of conciliar teaching bristles with phrases that need nuancing familiar to ecclesiologists. I cannot go into these because of my restricted scope. I will, however, clarify and re-interpret some key aspects which I believe have been mistakenly assumed to be present in the teaching of Vatican I. When these assumptions are corrected, significant limitations to the exercise of the infallible papal magisterium will emerge.

Let me list three of these assumptions:

First, regarding *what* the pope can infallibly teach: It has been assumed that the pope can teach any matter contained in the sources of revelation (Scripture and the Tradition that interprets the reality in Scripture) or relating to those sources. This means, for example, that the Pope can teach irreformably anything that pertains to faith in Scripture. He can teach with infallible certitude the meaning of any text that relates to doctrine. Conceivably he could teach irreformably the names of the authors of the various books and the dates of their composition. As long as a teaching related to faith is contained in some way in Scripture or Tradition, the pope can exercise his infallible magisterium with regard to it. This assumption underlies the classical treatments of infallibility.

Second, regarding the conditions for the exercise of the infallible magisterium: The pope has to make clear in some way while issuing a doctrinal teaching that he intends to fulfill these four conditions. Once he has made those conditions clear, his teaching is *ipso facto* irreformable. This is the way the theological manuals and Hans Küng view the matter.[8]

Third, regarding the role of bishops when the pope claims to teach irreformably: Since the pope's teaching is irreformable, by the very fact that he declares he has fulfilled the conditions, the only proper response of the bishops is immediate assent. I believe these assumptions are either wrong or have need of adjustment. These corrections will reveal in-built doctrinal limitations to the exercise of the papal infallible magisterium.

First, regarding *what* the pope can infallibly teach: My thesis is that the direct and primary object of infallibility is not any and all teaching pertaining to faith or morals but only those aspects of faith which are universally present. My discussion will first treat the meaning of the phrase "aspects of faith which are universally present" or its equivalent, "universal objective faith meanings." In subsequent sections, I will justify the assertion that only these aspects constitute the primary object of the pope's infallible magisterium.

What are Universal Faith Meanings? A universal meaning can be understood by contrasting it with a concept. Every true concept is universal in that it refers to abstract aspects of reality which can be grasped by all. Thus, I am now sitting in front of a computer. That aspect of my being and activity involved in my sitting before the computer is an abstraction, a partial intelligibility of my present being. Anyone grasping that aspect grasps a truth of my present being. Moreover, that same aspect can be grasped by other persons at different places and times, and it will represent for them a truth pertinent to this specific place and time. It will forever be true that I sat before this computer today. The concept reflecting this abstraction is truly universal.

However, that concept does not represent an aspect of objective reality, an intelligibility of my being, which is true of me at all moments of my existence. Tomorrow I shall be flying to New York. I shall not be sitting before the computer. It will not be true of me then or the next day to say that I am sitting before the computer. Accordingly, sitting before the computer does not represent a continuing aspect of my being; therefore, it is not a universal objective meaning.

What would be a universal objective meaning? Suppose I conceptualize the fact that I am culturally conditioned. This, like the concept of my sitting before the computer today, is a true concept. But there is a difference. This concept represents an intelligibility that is universally true of my being. I am culturally conditioned today; I shall be culturally conditioned tomorrow when I am flying to New York; I shall be culturally conditioned every day of my life no matter where I shall be. My being culturally conditioned is a universal objective meaning. It represents what is enduringly true of objective reality, not merely what is true of one or a few moments and places in time.

These notions can be applied to matters of faith. Contrast the statement "Jesus is risen" with the statement that "Jesus was born on December 25" or that "He was visited by Magi when an infant." The statement "Jesus is risen" represents a universal objective faith meaning. We believe it to be an enduring condition of his existence. Christ will always be risen and present to grace the world. However, even if we make the assumption that it is true that "Jesus was born on December 25" or that "He was visited by Magi when an infant," these statements merely articulate what happened at particular moments of time; they do not represent enduring objective faith meanings.

Why only universal objective faith meanings can be the object of defini-tion by the pope's infallible magisterium: the Church has long seen dog-mas as binding on all as a condition of salvation for all. This is ex-emplified in the theological notion that to be saved all must believe at the minimum that God exists and is a rewarder. Dogmas thus merit being called "saving truths."

But how does dogma save all? One possible answer is that God has es-tablished as a condition of salvation that certain propositions must be ac-cepted. These propositions have no intrinsic connection with salvation; rather, they are tests of our acceptance of the divine will; they are, as it were, hoops that God asks us to jump through to show we are fit for salva-tion. We embrace these propositions on faith in the divine testimony, and because we are obedient to the divine will, God rewards us with salvation. In this view, accepting doctrines is not intrinsic to the being-saved condi-tion. God could have set other conditions for salvation. For example, the divine will could have decided that those who are to be saved must all speak Latin or that they must believe in the existence of the Magi.

This crude notion goes counter to the long Catholic tradition which sees faith as intrinsically saving. It was recognized by St. Thomas that the act of faith saves because it terminates not in a proposition but in the reality of God.[9] What this means is that it is union with the reality of God and God's creation that saves us.

We are shaped by every relationship to reality, and it is the key central aspects of all reality that save us when we are united to them. Thus, to love God is intrinsically saving for all; to accept that God is pouring divine love upon us is intrinsically saving for all; to love one's neighbor is intrin-sically saving for all. This accounts for the fact that the eschatological condition of salvation is a total communion with God and all God's crea-tion. It will be the actual union to the totality of reality in depth which shall constitute salvation.

What then is the role of a faith proposition that saves? Simply this. It indicates partial aspects of the reality which saves. It is meant to guide our minds and hearts and hands toward union to the aspects of reality it represents. Each person is saved by encountering the persons, circumstances, and things surrounding him or her in ways that lead to the final communion of saints. A saving proposition in a specific circumstance indicates what one must think, how one must act, or what attitudes one must adopt in that particular setting.

Against this background, what is a truth that is saving for all? It can only be a proposition that represents some aspect of reality that confronts all persons at every moment, an aspect that is a universal condition of being. This is, of course, identical with the "universal objective faith meanings" which I have claimed is the direct object of the pope's infallible magisterium. Once one accepts this notion, one can immediately see why papal definitions are binding on all. They bind on all because they reflect reality which faces all.

The consequent connection between universality and irreformability: these features are correlatives. Precisely because a truth is universal in existence it is irreformable; by its nature it articulates what is true for all places and times. It will, thus, not have to be revised. Note the difference between what is merely true and what is irreformably true. It is true that I am here today and it will always be true that I was here today.

But my being here will not be true forever; for this is something merely true. As merely true it could never be proved conclusively two hundred years from now. But what is irreformably true today will always be true of reality; as such, it can be conclusively asserted two hundred years hence as having been true today. And so the date Christ was born may have been known certainly by his mother; but we cannot know that date with certainty now. That the human Christ was historically conditioned is a universal qualification of earthly existence. Hence, we can know it with certitude even after two millennia.[10]

What about factual objections to the thesis? We have doctrines that are not universal meanings in that they refer to events of a specific place and time, not to all places and all times. Examples are the doctrines of the Death and Resurrection of Christ and the Virginal Conception of Jesus.

My response is that we believe in these doctrines precisely in their universal import. We believe that the Christ who died as all must die so accepted the Father's will in death that he was raised and becomes universally present as Lord and Savior to all. That Christ physically died at a given place and time is not the object of faith. That he died and that his love unto death for us persists into his risen existence, and that as risen he is universally present Lord and Savior—there is the faith object.

The Virginal Conception is more complex. I believe that to understand this doctrine it must be seen against the background of the doctrines of the Assumption and the perpetual virginity of Mary. The Assumption of Mary refers to a universal condition of present existence. She joins the cohort that surrounds Christ as the Queen of all saints. She is present to all, and hence can be prayed to by all. Further, she exemplifies the risen condition which we are all called to share.

But who is the Mary who lives forever with God and pleads for us? She is a virginal person in all that she is, a condition that marked her whole life on earth and carries on into the afterlife. When we celebrate and honor Mary we honor her as she now is, as the prolongation and intensification of what she was on earth, the assumed (fulfilled) virgin.

Of course, everything in human existence has to begin at some particular time. Therefore, there was a moment when Christ died, when Mary conceived and gave birth. To deny such moments would be to deny the continuing states these moments initiated. Hence, the existence of these particular historical moments can be declared by the Church's infallible magisterium as necessary to protect the enduring objective faith meanings. This exemplifies the familiar notion of the so-called "secondary objects of infallibility." These secondary objects are truths that are necessary to protect the validity of the primary universal doctrines of faith.

Effect of the Thesis: If what I have stated is correct, the scope of the pope's infallible magisterium is much more restricted than has been assumed. It would seem that the pope *cannot* make definitive pronouncements about social situations, e.g., the correctness of proposed legislation. He *cannot* teach definitively with regard to Scripture in such matters as the date or authors of given books.[11]

Further, the pope cannot teach definitively in matters of concrete moral decisions. There are, I believe, abstract universal moral principles. But all concrete moral cases involve more than moral principles; and since these other factors (the moral capacity of the individual is the most noteworthy) are not universal but particular, the pope cannot pronounce infallibly on them or upon the specific moral decision to which they make an essential contribution. This explains why the conscience of the individual Christian has the final say in a concrete case. That conscience may fully accept the moral principles enunciated by the magisterium, but it alone can take into account the other factors contributing to a moral decision.[13]

Conditions for the Exercise of the Infallible Magisterium

As I have indicated, the manuals and Hans Küng believe that for the pope to exercise his infallible magisterium he need only declare that he is fulfilling the conditions laid down by Vatican I. On the contrary, with a number of other modern theologians, I have held that the pope must do more than declare that the conditions are fulfilled.[14] He must actually fulfill them. It is possible for a pope to claim to fulfill them and yet teach heresy because he has not actually done so. In that case, the medieval theologians recognized that he would *ipso facto* cease to be pope.

As far as I can tell, there has been little discussion on *why* the pope must fulfill these conditions. My own view is that these conditions all bespeak universality and that when they are fulfilled they refer to universal objective faith meanings *which of their nature are irreformable*: the pope must act as the head of the whole Church; he must be teaching a doctrine of faith and morals for all; he must be defining, that is, binding irrevocably for all time. Anyone who actually fulfilled comparable conditions of universality would utter irreformable truth. It is the pope who by his universal office is called at times to such an utterance officially.

The Role of Bishops when the Pope Claims to Teach Irreformably

Because it was assumed that the pope's teaching was irreformable by the mere fact that he indicated that he had fulfilled the conditions for the exercise of his infallible magisterium, many held that the only response appropriate for the bishops of the Church was immediate acceptance without question.

My own view is as follows. Whenever the pope indicates that he intends to teach infallibly, the presumption is that he has actually fulfilled the conditions. However, the bishops do a disservice to the Church if they rubber stamp papal teaching. This is not primarily because there is that slight possibility that the pope has not fulfilled the conditions. Rather, the function of all Church teaching is to illuminate and clarify what is already in faith experience and to facilitate decisions that flow from that illumination and clarification. Bishops know that when the pope fulfills the conditions for irreformable teaching, he is articulating what will resonate with the faith experience of the entire Church. Accordingly, they examine the faith of their respective Churches to detect the resonance of that faith with the pope's teaching.[15] This procedure not only deepens the unity of pope and bishops; it also provides a means by which further aspects of the truth may be unearthed by the bishops.

No pope should fear bishops who carefully examine irreformable papal teachings against the faith of their churches. The notion that the pope could teach irreformably what the vast majority of bishops disagree with is ridiculous. It is to suppose that the Holy Spirit guides only the pope and not the community of bishops also.

Meaning and Justification of
Merely Authentic Papal Teaching

The pope rarely claims to exercise his infallible magisterium. In most cases his teaching is what has been called "merely authentic." As Francis Sullivan, at the Gregorian University, indicates, the word "authentic" means that a teaching is "authoritative," that it stems from those who are endowed to teach with authority derived from Christ.[16] Hence, all teaching in the Church directed by the pope or bishops to the faithful at large, including the irreformable teaching mentioned in the prior section of this paper, is authentic teaching.

"Merely authentic teaching" is teaching by the pope or bishop which does not purport to be irreformable. In line with what I have said about the universality of irreformable teaching, I believe that teaching is "merely authentic" for any of three reasons. First, the content of the teaching may be erroneous. An example is the Church's acceptance of the permissibility of slavery as an institution. Second, the content of the teaching may lack universality; it does not reflect the faith of the whole Church but only the faith of limited culturally conditioned times and places.

Thus, the long proclaimed opposition to interest-taking (usury) represented an aspect of the faith life suitable to a non-commercial economy. Third, the content of the teaching may be universal, but its universal validity has not yet been seen as such by the Church's official teachers and the vast majority of the faithful. This third case is merely authentic by manner rather than by substance as in the first two cases.

My own view is that the word "official" perhaps best captures in secular terms the meaning of merely authentic teaching. Thus, the Supreme Court of the United States can be said to teach officially the meaning of the Constitution and the laws of Congress. No one claims that the judges teach infallibly; but when they sit, they render the official teaching, teaching which is to be followed by all because of the societal need for unity. What merely authentic papal teaching is to the Catholic Church, a Supreme Court legal interpretation is to the United States. Such teaching always maintains its official nature and always has the presumption of truth because of the authority from which it proceeds. But it may be mistaken. Accordingly, official teaching may be called "official truth" only with qualifications.

Analogous structures of official teachers are set up in various sectors of society. As Stephen Toulmin has asserted, each science has its own authoritative council of elders. At any given moment, a view is seen as acceptable because it gets the approval of a shifting group of recognized experts in the field. The views this group accepts are accounted as good science. What it rejects is beyond the pale. Rising young scientists have to impress this group and eventually become part of it as their elders leave it because of death or decline in reputation. Once young mavericks become accepted into the group, their views gain professional favor.[17] In short, every scientific endeavor has its own "magisterium." And what is declared to be objective truth in any science is not so much what shines by its own merit, but what passes muster with that "magisterium." Each science has its organ of "official truth," and it also has its multitude of young mavericks pushing toward a revision of "official truth."

The justification for a structure of official teachers seems to me to be evident. A truth shines by its own light only to those who have developed the ability to examine critically the area of reality the truth purports to reflect. An official teaching structure attempts to marshall a group of such persons and to provide, however imperfectly, for the updating provided by young mavericks. What no area of knowledge can accept as intelligent is the notion that every Tom, Dick, and Harriet should have the right to oppose or act against the teaching of the official "magisterium." The average person is unable to judge the validity of the quantum theory, the nature of the best cure for cancer, or the permissibility of *in vitro* fertilization.

Limits Regarding the Merely Authentic Teaching Power of the Pope

There are a number of limits surrounding official papal teaching. I shall address two of them. First, limits that derive from what the pope (or his curia) teaches and, second, limits deriving from the obligation of bishops to receive that teaching.

Limits deriving from what the pope teaches: If the pontiff (or his curia for him) is teaching as the head of the whole Church then he must be attempting to articulate what pertains to the universal faith. Accordingly, he is held to garner what he teaches not from the Roman diocesan tradition, not from his personal life, but from the developing Tradition of the whole Church. Accordingly, when a pope does creative theology (as with Pius XII) or when he meditates on the Scriptures (as with John Paul II's recent meditation on women,[18] John Paul's exegesis of Ephesians and his seeming extension of original sin to Eve) his new teaching should be respected, but not made *ipso facto* into teaching binding on all as official.

Certainly the pope has a right to express his personal opinions. It is irrational to demand that he restrict his life to uttering only what is in the tradition of the universal Church. However, such personal opinions do not by the mere fact that they are his become binding on all. Hence, experts can disagree with his specific exegesis of biblical texts in appropriate fora. So may bishops, again in appropriate fora. Such disagreement is not dissent; for dissent is disagreement with authentic teaching, not with personal opinion.

In terms of modern circumstances, this also applies to members of the pope's curia. Cardinal Ratzinger, for example, is entitled to his own opinion on theological matters. He published his particular views in the past, and he is still publishing them. But I look with some misgivings on the way we theologians like to quote the earlier Ratzinger against the Ratzinger of the present. This procedure can obscure the fact that many of his views, both past and present, are his personal views, and as such they have no special stature just because he now happens to be the head of the Congregation for the Doctrine of the Faith.

Limits Deriving from Reception of Papal Teaching by Bishops

Reception of papal teaching by the Church is the process by which members of the Church seek and find the degree to which the teaching corresponds with their living faith. When a papal teaching resonates fully with the faith of the persons who hear it that teaching is simply accepted. If the teaching seems to be somewhat out of accord with the recipients' living faith, then they must question the quality of their faith. However, should the dissonance continue and be supported by others, then there emerges the possibility that the papal teaching itself is not entirely accurate. In any case, one does a disservice to the Church by pretending to accept fully a papal teaching one does not see. I am not talking about dissent; I am talking about a desire for truth that leads a Catholic to say of a papal teaching, "I do not see. Show me."

Such reception is first of all by bishops. They should listen to papal teaching with respect and respond with a firm "Yes" when that teaching corresponds to the faith they discern in their Churches and know from their history. But their "Yes" should not be automatic. It can happen that they experience elements which lead them to think that the papal or curial articulation is in some measure inadequate. In that case they should express their misgivings, not to the media, but to the Holy See. For their office is to witness to the faith of their Churches, not to be a mere repeater of the teaching of the Holy See. Only a theology which views bishops as mere representatives of the Holy See can make this mistake.[19]

It seems evident that for much of recent history bishops acted as if the only proper response to merely authentic papal or curial teaching was an automatic assent. I believe this is one extreme.

The other extreme would be immediate episcopal skepticism about papal teaching or a downright dissenting attitude. I believe that the middle position demands that bishops adopt a docile stance which seeks for the correlation between the faith of their Churches with the pontiff's doctrine. If such a correlation is partially absent, then the loyal response is to make known this fact to the Holy See. This mode of acting is not dissent; rather, it is a recognition that the truth is represented not by the bishops alone, not by the pope alone, but by the pope in union with the bishops.

I am encouraged by the fact that since the beginning of Vatican II bishops have haltingly but steadily begun to recognize in practice that they have a right and an obligation to contribute positively to the formulation of true doctrine in their responses to papal or curial teaching. This fact, to my mind, is far more significant for the modification and correction of possible mistakes by the papal magisterium than the right of dissent claimed by theologians.

Lest my assertion of optimism seem unwarranted, let me close with several examples of bishops responses which have produced qualification and even rejection of papal teaching. When taken together they impressively indicate that both bishops and popes are coming to realize that an automatic yes response to papal teaching is not loyalty to Christ.

The first and most important example occurred at Vatican II, when the bishops were presented with a series of documents by the papal curia. As is well known, these documents were largely rejected as starting points for discussion, and new documents were drawn up. No claim was ever made that this was disloyal dissent.

I have a suspicion that this activity of the Council Fathers more than any other helped to restore to the psyche of bishops the recognition that they are immediate witnesses to the faith rather than mere mediate witnesses through the pope. We may never adequately assess the profound and lasting effect of this response to curial teaching upon the world's bishops.

As a second example, on October 3, 1984, the Congregation for Divine Worship issued a document authorizing bishops to allow use of the Tridentine Mass under special circumstances.[20] A few weeks later at the Vatican, representatives of thirty-two English-speaking episcopal conferences responded to the Congregation's document with "grave concern, regret and dismay." The English-speaking bishops declared that the concession made by the Congregation "appears to be a movement away from the ecclesiology of the Second Vatican Council," . . . "seems to give support to those who have resisted the liturgical renewal," . . . and appears to subvert the responsibility of episcopal conferences and the Holy See itself over liturgical change by giving each local bishop the right to make decisions about the use of the Tridentine Mass. What appeared to upset the bishops was the fact that the congregation seemed to "violate the collegial sense of the worldwide episcopate, 98 percent of whom, when asked by the congregation on this question, responded that this was not a problem in the Church but rather only the concern of a tiny minority who have contrived to create the impression that it is a much greater issue than in fact it is."[21]

I need not attempt to amplify the facts of this case. It is evident, no matter what one's views on the Tridentine Mass, that in this instance the members of many episcopal conferences regarded themselves not as mere obedient servants of the Vatican, but as genuine contributors to the formation of Vatican teaching and to its practical implementation.

Third, on August 6, 1984, the Sacred Congregation for the Doctrine of the Faith issued a rather negative instruction on the theology of liberation.[22] On March 22, 1986, partially as the result of an intervention by the Brazilian hierarchy, the same congregation issued the more positive "Instruction on Christian Freedom and Liberation."[23]

Finally, the Holy See recently issued a Draft Statement on Episcopal Conferences.[24] The United States Conference set in motion a process to examine the document. At its conclusion it replied to the Vatican that its view was that the document was inadequate as a starting point for discussing the role of episcopal conferences.

These few examples illustrate a growing consciousness on the part of bishops that they are direct witnesses of the faith of their Churches, not mere duplicators of papal teaching. As witnesses to the faith of their individual Churches they contribute significantly to the exercise of the pope's charism of universal teacher. Their role in responding to papal teaching, though it cannot be stated in terms of *legal* rights, helps refine and even correct papal understanding. Accordingly, the courageous exercise of their role constitutes an important limitation on merely authentic papal teaching authority.

To conclude, it is a mistake to think that the pope's authority is so unlimited that in teaching he is responsible to God alone. Pope Paul VI once suggested to the theological commission working on the Constitution on the Church that it include in Chapter Three a formula stating that the pope is "accountable to the Lord alone." The commission rejected the formula based on the following reasoning.

> It is an oversimplified formula. The Roman Pontiff is also bound to revelation itself, to the fundamental structure of the Church, to the sacraments, to the definitions of earlier councils, and other obligations too numerous to mention.[25]

It is a measure of the greatness of Paul VI that he immediately ceased to push his suggestion.

To sum up, I have indicated in this paper that in the very nature of truth and of the collegial structure of the Church's episcopacy there are factors which limit the extent of the pope's teaching authority. I have highlighted these few limiting factors not merely because they have ecumenical importance but also because I believe that if they are put into operation they will assist the pope to proclaim the truth that makes all of us free.

Notes

1. A reading of J. M. R. Tillard, *The Bishop of Rome* (Wilmington: Glazier, 1983) will substantiate the official reluctance to treat the obligations of the papacy and the limits of papal prerogatives.

2. For a concise expressing of such malaise on the part of Lutherans, see *Lutherans and Catholics in Dialogue: Vol V, Papal Primacy and the Universal Church* (Minneapolis: Augsburg, 1974), p. 13.

3. "Open Questions in Dogma Considered by the Institutional Church as Definitively Answered," *Journal of Ecumenical Studies* 15/2 (Spring 1978): 218-223.

4. *The Limits of the Papacy* (New York: Crossroad, 1987).

5. As of today I have no publication information from Graymoor.

6. My fundamental criticism of Granfield's book (see note 4) is that he relies on voluntary renunciation by the pope of some of his powers. See my review in *Commonweal* (Nov 6, 1987) p. 634.

7. D.S. 3073, 3074.

8. Hans Küng, *Infallible? An Inquiry* (Garden City, New York: Doubleday, 1971), pp. 101-5.

9. See *Summa Theologiae*, IIa IIae, q.1, a.2, ad.2. "*Actus autem credentis non terminatur ad enuntiabile, sed ad rem.*"

10. Incidentally, this explanation helps clarify the natural infallibility of the human mind. It suggests that anyone can teach infallibly what is truly universal. Accordingly, anyone can teach infallibly that all human views are partial, that all human persons are culturally conditioned, and that no human being can understand without prior experience. This indicates that infallibility is not some extra-human gift of God. It is a human quality as applied to faith. This seemingly rather revolutionary view is in accord with the modern understanding that all revelation is in the humanity of Christ. Hence, all revealed truth must partake of the human.

11. Of course, in line with what was said in the prior paragraph, a pope can make an irreformable statement about the author or dating of a text to the extent that such is needed to protect universal faith meanings. Thus, a pope might deny a chronology which would date the existence of the biblical Christ to 150 C.E. because such a chronology would effectively deny that Christianity and its faith is derived from Christ.

12. Raymond Brown, *The Critical Meaning of the Bible* (New York: Paulist, 1981), p. 40 asserts, "To the best of my knowledge the Roman Catholic Church has never defined the literal sense of a single passage of the Bible." By "literal sense" Brown means the meaning intended by the author. My text is consistent with Brown's view but goes beyond it. What he asserts has not occurred, I maintain cannot occur.

13. Before concluding this section on the thesis that the pope can definitively teach directly only universally existing aspects of faith life, I would suggest that Vatican II went a long way toward enunciating a parallel doctrine with regard to biblical inerrancy. As is well known, it was frequently taught by popes up to Vatican II that the Bible was without error. Moreover, the original drafts of The *Dogmatic Constitution on Divine Revelation* (*Dei Verbum*) maintained that Scripture was absolutely free of error. This meant that, *understood in context*, every single biblical assertion, even of the most specific detail, was guaranteed to be

true by reason of divine inspiration. However, these original drafts were all rejected largely as the result of an intervention by Cardinal König on October 2, 1964. The Cardinal pointed out numerous errors of detail in the biblical text. In the end of the official text of *Dei Verbum* #11 declared that "the books of Scripture, firmly, faithfully, and without error, teach *that truth which God, for the sake of our salvation,* wished to see confided to the Sacred Scriptures." (Emphasis mine.) The text of *Dei Verbum* is taken from Austin Flannery, *Vatican Council II,* Vol. I (Collegeville, Minnesota: Liturgical Press, 1984), pp. 757.

On the history of this text on inerrancy see the detailed account of Alois Grillmeier in Herbert Vorgrimler, ed. *Commentary on the Documents of Vatican II* (New York: Herder and Herder, 1969), Vol III, pp. 199-215.

14. For a discussion of this question and for a reference to theologians who hold this view (e.g., Ratzinger, Kasper, Congar, et al.) see Francis Sullivan, *Magisterium* (New York: Paulist, 1983), pp. 106-109 and the appended note #32 on pp. 224-25.

15. A classic example of such episcopal response to papal teaching was that of the bishops at Chalcedon to the teaching of Pope Leo the Great. For a nuanced treatment of this issue see W. de Vries, *Orient et Occident* (Paris: Cerf, 1974), pp. 126-49.

16. Sullivan, *Magisterium,* pp. 26-28.

17. Stephen Toulmin, *Human Understanding,* Vol 1, *The Collective Use and Evolution of Concepts* (Princeton: Princeton University Press, 1972), pp. 262-300.

18. For John Paul's apostolic letter "Mulieris Dignitatem," see *Origins,* Vol. 18, No. 17 (October 6, 1988): 263-83.

19. That the bishop is not a mere representative of the Holy See was acknowledged in *Lumen Gentium* #27. The point was delightfully made in a letter sent by Archbishop Pio Laghi to a priest friend of mine. The priest had complained in writing to the Delegate that many of the people who were criticizing Archbishop Hunthausen to the Holy See did not acknowledge that the Archbishop was the sole representative of the Holy See in Seattle. The priest was surprised to receive an answer from the Delegate stating, "I wish to correct your theology. Archbishop Hunthausen is not the representative of the Holy See in Seattle. I am the representative of the Holy See in the United States. Archbishop Hunthausen is the representative ativeativeativeativeativeof Jesus Christ in Seattle." I do not have the letter. The wording given is from memory.

20. The text of this document is printed in *Origins* Vol 14, No. 19 (October 25, 1984): 290.

21. *Origins,* Vol. 14, No. 21 (November 8, 1984): 334-45.

22. *Origins,* Vol. 14, No. 13 (September 13, 1984): 195-204.

23. *Origins,* Vol. 15, No. 44 (April 17, 1986): 715-28.

24. *Origins,* Vol. 17, No. 43 (April 7, 1988): 731-37.

25. See Patrick Granfield, *The Limits of the Papacy* (New York: Crossroad, 1987), pp. 62-63.

5

Feminist Analysis and Church Authority: Reflections on Recent North American Episcopal Statements on Women

Mary Ellen Sheehan, I.H.M.
St. Michael's College, University of Toronto

The feminist movement is complex and prolific. It impacts explosively on traditional knowledge and practice in art, literature, education, the natural and social sciences, philosophy and theology.[1] Although feminist analysis is far from coherent with respect to its specific objectives and methods, its goal is nothing less than the transformation of culture, a mission about which it has no question, because of the increasing consciousness of sexism in our contemporary world. Most feminists would agree with Jane Flax, a political scientist at Howard University, that "a fundamental goal of feminist theory is to analyze gender relations: how gender relations are constituted and experienced and how we think or, equally important, do not think about them."[2]

Feminist analysis includes at least two moments, variantly named either as descriptive and prescriptive, or deconstructive and constructive, or as critical retrieval and reconstruction. Adopting the language of the first pair, the *descriptive* phase includes an historical and contemporary analysis of the assumptions grounding cultural male domination, as well as certain aspects of the Enlightenment Period,[3] which led to class and gender privelege. In particular, feminist analysis uncovers the hitherto almost universally accepted power of patriarchy to define the nature and role of women, and it lays bare the devastating consequences of this. Exclusion, marginalization, objectification, and subordination to the male as normative of human personhood are four such corollaries of patriarchy.

The *prescriptive* element of feminist analysis aims at achieving "a critical distance on existing gender arrangements" in order to "clear a space in which reevaluating and altering our existing gender arrangements may become more possible."[4] This phase stresses the critical "re-membering" of women's experience to history through the retrieval of hidden, repressed, or forgotten sources. It also entails *political action* to restructure relationships.

Needless to say, Christian theology has not been unaffected by contemporary cultural feminism. Indeed Christian inspired theory and practice is already imaginatively at work to shape the radical transformationist agenda of contemporary feminism. Christian feminism is ecumenical in nature, and it is becoming increasingly evident that theologians and pastoral workers with a feminist consciousness are engaged worldwide in the work of cultural and ecclesial transformation.[5] Along with their sisters and brothers of other churches, Roman Catholic theologians and pastoral workers have made great contributions to the descriptive and prescriptive tasks of feminist analysis,[6] and judging from the increased presence of women in theological and pastoral studies engaged in feminist critique, there is every reason to believe that this committed work will continue, unto the endtimes if necessary.

But having made these general points about cultural and Christian feminism, the task I have set for myself in this paper is not a further commentary on the very important results of this work. Rather, I want to focus on some recent North American Roman Catholic Bishops' statements on women. My guiding question is: how are the bishops exercising their teaching office with respect to current issues on women? Are there any signs yet of transformational theology and pastoral practice on the episcopal level with regard to gender relations?

First, I will comment in a general way on the contexts of these statements. Secondly, I will identify some cultural and theological influences at work in the documents that show some promise for widening the basis of theological reasoning and practice regarding our church's tradition on women. Because of the limits of this paper, I will concentrate on the texts of some Canadian bishops and make reference to the parallel development among some Unites States bishops. Thirdly, I will point to problems in these documents and how a feminist analysis promises to *pester*[7] for some time the nature and exercise of authority in the church.

I borrow the image of *pestering* from a colleague of mine at Toronto, Mary Jo Leddy, who wrote an article in the *Catholic New Times*, a meditation on the effect of the Canaanite woman on the consciousness of Jesus.

Many feminist theologians would question the significance of the approach I am taking, either because they judge all present structures, and particularly hierarchical ones, as irreformably patriarchal or because they hold that only women can speak about women's experience. These feminist thinkers would hold that since talk about gender relations presupposes women speaking of it *from* and *with* their own voices and since presently women have no official voice in the church, then Roman Catholic bishops, all of whom presently are men, can have nothing valid to say about the subject.

I must say that I share some of the thinking entailed in these positions, but I also believe, as do several other Catholic feminist theologians,[8] that we can retrieve and invoke critically the liberative strands within the Christian tradition to effect, *in action*, concrete historical transformation of the church and culture. Thus, I proceed in hope with my task.

Since 1971, Canadian bishops have issued about twelve public statements on women in church and society and United States bishops have published about twenty such texts. These statements include interventions at Roman synods, Pastoral Letters issued to their local dioceses, reports on the work and results of Ad Hoc Committees on Women in Church and Society established by the Bishops' respective National Conferences, public addresses, and media interviews. In addition, the United States bishops are of course engaged in developing a Pastoral Letter entitled, *Partners in the Mystery of Redemption: A Pastoral Response to Women's Concerns for Church and Society*. The first draft has been published and is now being widely circulated for study and evaluation.[9] Although I cannot offer a full analysis of these documents in this paper,[10] I can point out the cultural and theological influences at work.

Cultural and Theological Influences at Work in Developing a More Truthful View of Women

A.The Canadian Bishops

1. The 1971 Synod in Rome

In preparation for the 1971 Synod of Bishops in Rome with its two-fold theme of the *Ministerial Priesthood* and *Justice in the World,* the Canadian Bishops engaged in a dialogue with women over several recommendations formulated from women's groups in the Archdiocese of Edmonton. Among other requests, these proposals asked that discrimination against women be removed from Canon Law, that women be given equal rights in the church, that women be admitted to ordination, that the clergy be taught to respect the inherent dignity of women in all domains, and that there be greater solidarity with women working outside the home, especially those suffering from social injustice.[11]

I learned something from a dear old professor in Louvain, who said that whenever there is a positive statement of something—he talked about this in terms of Councils—it means that the opposite has been going on in practice. So just take these proposals and understand that the need to say this indicates something other than what they state has been going on.

During their Plenary Assembly in September, 1971, the bishops agreed to raise the topic of women in both themes, that is, in the discussion of ministerial priesthood and also justice in the world.

George Cardinal Flahiff, then Archbishop of Winnipeg, represented the Canadian bishops and addressed the synod assembly briefly and unambiguously. Flahiff first asserted the need to re-examine the scriptural and historical arguments preventing the admission of women to public ministry in the church and also the need to eliminate all passages in the Code of Canon Law that reflect the position of the natural inferiority of women to men. Then, noting Vatican II's "categorical statements against all discrimination against women in the church . . . and the fact that no notable effort has been made to implement this teaching," Flahiff posed two questions:

> 1. Given the growing recognition both in law and in fact of the equality of women with men and the recognition likewise of the injustice of all discrimination against women, should we not raise the question whether women too are to have a place

in the sacred ministries of the Church as they exist or as they are developing?

2. With the emergence of new forms of ministries, under the direction of the Holy Spirit, to serve a society that is developing so rapidly, can we foresee or at least allow for ministries for women that are even better adapted than the traditional ones to their nature, their gifts, their competence both in the society and in the church of the modern world of which *Gaudium et Spes* spoke so eloquently?

As a practical step, he urged the immediate establishment of a gender-mixed Papal Commission to study the question of the ministries of women in the church, observing that despite a centuries-old social tradition against a ministry of women in the church, we are convinced that the signs of the times (and one of those signs is that already many women perform many pastoral services and with great success) strongly urge a study at least both of the present situation and of possibilities for the future.

Now that Commission did exist and one of the outflows of that was the famous *Inter Insigniores*, the declaration on the admission of women to ordination, which I think would more aptly be called the declaration on the *exclusion* of women from ordination. That was one result. Flahiff further claimed that unless such a study is begun at once, the bishops could indeed find themselves "behind the course of events."[12] Now, he is Canadian, and I am an American woman reading this, and I remember one other time hearing "when in the course of human events"—so a phrase, though it is a simple one, gives one a lot to think about.

2. The 1980 Synod in Rome

The Canadian bishops continued their proclamation on equality for women in the church at the 1980 Roman synod on the Family. Bishop Robert Lebel of Valleyfield, Québec, addressed the Synod stating that it is:

out of fidelity to the Word of God that the church ought to recognize as positive the modern feminist movement. It is a question, as a whole, of progress within civilization and it is one more step in the coming of the kingdom.[13]

Further, Lebel claimed, the church should not be lagging behind positive cultural developments but rather be boldly prophetic in word and action in promoting all forms of liberation. The situation of the oppression of women, both in society and in the church, is a sinful one that must be denounced and corrected. Lebel pointed out, for instance, as inherently sexist, the church's current practice of prohibiting females from altar service. Bishops, he cautioned, should spare themselves the embarrassment of having to defend such unreasonable regulations.

Nor is it enough to condemn sexism. Women must become co-responsible for the broader pastoral activities of the church, including participation in planning and decision-making. Bishops are called, not to obscure the word of God by reticence, but rather to welcome the ministry of women as an opportunity for the church.[14]

3. The 1983 Synod in Rome

The 1983 Synod on Reconciliation became the occasion for the Canadian bishops to express themselves even more strongly on the question of women in the church. In his Synod Intervention, Archbishop Louis Albert Vachon of Québec City recalled that the church has indeed been prophetic in its recent teachings on justice and on women. He warned, however, that these appeals of the church to the world for the advancement of the status of women are on the point of losing all impact unless the recognition of women as full members becomes simultaneously a reality within the church itself.

Reflecting on reconciliation as the way to realize a new humanity in Christ, Vachon made two further points.

First, he insisted on the necessity for men and women to listen to each other and in particular to understand the pervasiveness of sexism. Vachon asked his brother bishops to "recognize the ravages of sexism and our own male appropriation of church institutions and numerous aspects of the christian life," including language and other practices, as a way toward overcoming archaic conceptions of women. Secondly, Vachon declared the need for all to be opened anew to the Spirit of God for individual and collective conversion so that we can "discover what we must change in order to bring about the recognition of women as having the same full membership status as men."

4. Bishop Bernard Hubert, Pastoral Letter, December 1984

Bishop Hubert, from the diocese of St-Jean-Longueuil, which is near the diocese of Montréal, wrote a pastoral letter to his diocese in response to this issue. In the diocese of Québec a very active level of dialogue had begun between women in small groups and diocesan structures. This diocese has undergone a kind of de-clericalization, a "quiet revolution," as it is called. In the theological schools and pastoral institutes there, the largest percentage of students are lay people, men and women.

Hubert appeals to our theological tradition to legitimate his critique. Feminism, he says, is focused on justice. There is a moral imperative to correct the sin of sexism. The truth of universal salvation in Christ is made real in human struggle, including women's, for the historical Jesus laid claim to the equality of each person as made in God's own image. In the Trinity, Hubert recalls, there is no relation of inequality, no servitude, no domination, no exploitation. Indeed, the full equality of men and women in concrete mutuality is *required* as a sign of God's own transcendence.

Hubert acknowledges that there will be conflict and ambiguity in the process toward mutuality between men and women in the church. What is refreshingly hopeful in his theology of the church is that it includes *struggle*. Human struggle, he recognizes, is not exempt from "the sin which feeds injustice and exploitation," but neither is it without the grace to further the Kingdom through the realization of equality in the relationship of men and women. Vatican II has called the whole people of God to unceasing renewal. "Fortunately," Hubert recalls, ". . . the Church has all the freedom it needs to call itself into question again and again. Through all the changes of this world, it seeks and finds its Savior."[15]

5. Bishop Remi De Roo, A Public Address, October, 1986

Addressing a Washington, D.C., conference on *Women in the Church* in October, 1986, Bishop Remi De Roo of the Diocese of Victoria argued for change from a theological and pastoral view of Vatican II similar to that of Bishop Hubert. But he made two additional points worth highlighting here, namely, the need for depth social analysis of sexism and for invoking a renewed pneumatology in our efforts to realize the equality of women.

Like Hubert, De Roo sees the need to construct an alternate world view by the recovery of our broader theological tradition on the Trinity, the Church, and Christ as prophetic proclaimer of a discipleship of equals. He also invokes our tradition on the holy and creative presence of the Spirit of God. Real assent to the reality of the Holy Spirit, De Roo asserts, would be a humbling but revitalizing experience for the church, one that would most likely imply that gender can no longer be a determinant of fittingness for public ministry.

With respect to any cavalier dismissal of the question of women and ordination, De Roo asked: Is not the church's credibility being irreparably harmed? Are not ecumenical initiatives being adversely affected? Is not true justice being blocked? In fact, may it not be a time for the entire church to experience and to test the possible call from the Spirit to women for ordination?

De Roo's attitude in this public address is more open and exploratory than closed and decided, more oriented toward the future than toward the past, and more confident than not in the presence and gifts of the Holy Spirit in the whole church. He is also realistic about the present, recalling that we are a long way from a genuine converted consciousness on women's questions.[16]

6. The Synod on the Laity in Rome, October, 1987

In his intervention, Archbishop James M. Hayes of Halifax expressed clearly and directly that the theme of the laity and the "mission of the church at the beginning of the 21st century . . ." is an urgent one.

God calls us to have done with violence, injustice and discrimination, and to weed them out of the field of human history. We must endeavor together to respond to the life-threatening questions of our time: the search for peace, the awesome potential of biogenetics, the massive suffering imposed on the poor by international debt and the displacement of people, the challenge of a secular culture.

To this end, Hayes made a very concrete proposal. He asked for the accredited admission of laity, religious, and clergy at all future Synods, and, further, that there be movement toward a more comprehensive "synodal process," a proposal made by the Canadian bishops at the previous Synod on Vatican II in 1985.[17]

If indeed the church is *communio*, Hayes argued, then there is the need for constant dialogue among the members, even when there are difficulties, for "where real consultation and participation occur the Holy Spirit leads us through a kind of conversion . . ." that renews the dynamism and direction of the church's mission.[18]

At the same Synod, Archbishop Jean-Guy Hamelin of Rouyn-Noranda, Québec, also struck a chord of urgency in his intervention on women, saying that the very credibility of the church as witness is at stake if the equality of women is not recognized in representation and decision-making, in access to real pastoral responsibilities, and in the removal of all institutionalized inequality in canon law. Further, he was fearless in stating that the question of the ordination of women must be pursued, particularly since "the reasoning used so far to explain the reservation of sacred orders to men has not seemed convincing, especially not to young people."

B. The United States Bishops

Since 1974, besides work done at the national level by the National Conference of Catholic Bishops, there have been at least ten Pastoral Letters on women issued by United States bishops to their respective dioceses. Many of them contain natural law and theological reflections similar to those developed in the Canadian bishops' statements. In some cases, they are richer statements theologically and most of them propose strategies and concrete action steps for their dioceses. In this paper, we choose only a few of them to locate developments parallel to the Canadian bishops.

1. Archbishop Raymond Hunthausen, Pastoral Letter, 1980

Archbishop Raymond Hunthausen of Seattle stressed themes of salvation, equality of discipleship and conversion in his 1980 Pastoral Letter. He stated:

> Jesus gave a prominent place to women: all are called to equal roles as disciples. Only later in the Greek-Jewish world are women restricted. The relationship of liberation to salvation permeates the New Testament, the process of liberation is in the service of salvation, which reaches its climax in the final triumph of the Kingdom.

Hunthausen called for reflection on four themes concerning women in the church:

A. Salvation is offered to all, on the same terms, irrespective of race, sex or prior affiliations.

B. Sin is a condition affecting all equally, and consequently, there is a universal need for forgiveness and reconciliation.

C. The Incarnation is the human becoming of God in history. That Jesus became male is not the primary significance of the Incarnation.

D. Conversion is the process each must undergo in becoming the new person through faith and baptism. A new version of church, a renewed sense of mission and community, impel each and every person to inquire: What does a Church look like that is whole, just, and moving toward full incarnation of the Kingdom?[19]

Hunthausen urges the implementation of some nine actions in his diocese, including the elimination of sexist language and imagery from diocesan and parish publications, equal access for women to theological and pastoral education according to their capacities, and the active recruitment of qualified women to exercise a wide range of pastoral ministries in the diocese.

Stressing themes similar to Hunthausen's, Archbishop Peter Gerety issued a pastoral letter in 1980 which called on the people of his diocese to see the equality of women as a matter of injustice calling for deep conversion.

2. Bishops Victor Balke and Raymond Lucker, Joint Pastoral Letter, 1981

Two Minnesota bishops, Bishop Victor Balke of Crookston and Bishop Raymond Lucker of New Ulm, issued a joint Pastoral Letter in October, 1981. They situated their reflections within an understanding of Christian humanism that calls for a Gospel based commitment to the dignity and equality of all persons which must lead to "changes in structures, customs, institutions and relationships" for the good of all, and they were very direct and clear in naming the evil of sexism.

> Sexism, directly opposed to Christian humanism and feminism, is the erroneous belief or conviction or attitude that one sex, female or male, is superior to the other in the very order of creation or by the very nature of things. When anyone believes that men are inherently superior to women or that women are inherently superior to men, then he or she is guilty of sexism. Sexism is a moral and social evil. It is not the truth of the biological, sociological or psychological sciences, nor is it the truth of the Gospel. Sexism is a lie. It is a grievous sin, diminished in its gravity only by indeliberate ignorance or by pathological fear.

By contrast, the two bishops teach, was Jesus' attitude from which he "related to women with a marvelous inner freedom" recognizing their full humanity and personhood. Jesus "neither demeaned them nor divinized them—two extreme and inhuman ways of relating to women (ways women have historically experienced)," both of which have prevented "them from being full participants, equal to men, in the human enterprise."

In an effort to overcome the sexism that exists in all of us individually and in the structures of the church, these bishops propose a very thorough guide to examining our consciences. With regard to individual attitudes, they propose twelve questions, some of which include: Do I ever make disparaging remarks about women or react approvingly when others make such remarks? Do I stereotype women in any way or approve—even by silence—of statements that do stereotype them? Do I willingly listen to women when they speak about their status in the church and in society? Does it bother me when others speak of God as maternal as well as paternal?

In regard to pastoral practices, they pose another set of twelve questions, which include: Do my diocese and/or parish and school pay a just salary to women employees, a salary equal to men in similar positions? Does my diocese and/or parish provide a known and approachable forum for women to speak on issues especially relevant to them? Does my diocese and/or parish use inclusive language in its publications and communications and in the liturgy wherever possible? The bishops plead for change in attitudes and pastoral practices as a matter of justice and a measure of our fidelity to the Gospel.[20]

3. Bishop Matthew Clark, Pastoral Letter, 1982.

In a lengthy and theologically powerful Pastoral Letter issued in April, 1982, Bishop Matthew Clark of Rochester, New York, links women's painful experiences with oppression and exclusion to the need for conversion and reconciliation. Only by facing this challenging reality with the help of the Holy Spirit will we grow "toward the full stature of Christ." Bishop clark argues for the inclusive roles of women in the church as prophets, teachers, and preachers of the Gospel as well as leadership in pastoral care and governance.

Like Bishops Balke and Lucker, Clark concludes his letter with a series of challenging observations and calls for action. He offers eight reflections on discriminatory attitudes toward women, and he calls for repentance over the past, conversion regarding the present, and committed perseverance against the temptation to quit or otherwise withdraw from the concrete process of realizing women's full equality in the church. He also outlines twelve action steps toward a reconstructed future, some of which include: the full admission of qualified women to all ministries not requiring ordination; scholarships for women to study at the local seminary and other institutions; continuing research by theologians and biblical scholars on all questions related to the issues of women; the use of inclusive language; the continuing education of priests on women in the church, sexism and clericalism; team ministry through conferences which include qualified women in planning and presentation.

This review of some North American Roman Catholic bishops' statements on women has shown a steady and consistent public commitment to dealing with women's issues in the church and society which I believe manifests, to some measure at least, a clearly discernable appropriation of the prophetic character of their Episcopal Office. Their statements show a rich reflection, sourced in recovering aspects of our biblical and theological tradition as well as in welcoming contemporary cultural developments on gender relations, that show promise for redress and reconstruction in the church and society.

On public record, the bishops have acknowledged the women's movement as a positive and permanent feature of our contemporary consciousness. They have condemned sexism as a moral and social evil, and they have advocated an egalitarian partnership of men and women in the church. They have argued theologically that women are indeed a sign of God in history, fully equal to men, and further that their full membership in the church in theory and in practice is necessary for the truthfulness of the church itself as a credible prophetic witness to the liberating love of God as given to us in Jesus Christ and the Holy Spirit.

Issues Promising to Pester the Nature and Exercise of Authority in the Church

Despite this remarkable public proclamation and commitment to women's concerns in the church and society, a number of issues arise from a close reading of the bishop's statement that will continue to nag at the edges, or perhaps even at the center, of church authority. How much further will the church have to exercise its freedom and trust in calling itself into question? I would like to raise five such matters from reflecting on these episcopal documents.

1. Patriarchy, Power, and Sexism

The first concerns the degree of social analysis that is operative in the bishops' thought. With one exception (De Roo), there is no mention, for instance, in any of the statements of the concept of patriarchy and power and the extent to which real authority in the church still operates from patriarchal assumptions and practices. To what extent has the very hierarchical character of the church evolved from the presuppositions of patriarchy and is still dependent upon it? Until patriarchy is eradicated, there will still be subordination of one group to another and thus some form of exclusion and oppression. Sexism, in any of its forms, could still exist in a non-patriarchal society or institution, but it is *certain* to remain in any institution that continues to be patriarchal. The bishops and others in the church still have the formidable task of elaborating a biblical and theological justification for hierarchy which would be freed from its patriarchal theory and practice. Until this is done, sexism will continue to plague the church.

2. Democratic Values and Hierarchical Structures

No one would argue that a democratic institutional structure guarantees the actualization of justice and equality. Nevertheless, the theoretical and practical gains of democratically organized societies do exist as a pressure on hierarchical institutions. Values such as the right to assembly, the right to a voice in the affairs affecting basic human rights, the right to participation in the shaping of one's destiny and the common good, the rights to dissent and to vote challenge a theology touting the church as organized hierarchically by divine intent. Can the democratic elements which the bishops honor and use be absorbed locally, nationally, and universally in a hierarchically organized church?[21]

3. An Egalitarian Partnership or Reciprocal Complementarity?

The North American bishops that we have reviewed use some powerful phrases in referring to the status of women in the church. They proclaim that women must have the same full membership status as men; they speak of a discipleship of equals; they advocate the establishment of new bonds of equality in an egalitarian partnership. They do not, however, describe in any detail the precise meaning of these phrases. They could be understood to mean a full and equal reciprocal relationship based on a full and equal participation in rights, responsibilities and power. Or they could be understood as equal in dignity at the order of creation, but unequal at the level of functions, roles, and gifts.

If the latter is intended, then inequality remains. Insofar as women are judged *a priori* not to have certain gifts for the exercise of authority, inequality remains. What results is a relationship that cannot be equal either at the level of practice or at the level of theory.

All papal documents on women to date have excluded women from full participation in the life of the church, based not on their personhood which is fully equal to men's, but rather on their gender which makes them unfit for certain roles in the church.

4. Women as Necessary Sign of God's Image and Transcendence and Their Exclusion from Ordination

The Vatican Declaration, *Inter Insigniores*, issued on October 15, 1976, contains a summary of the biblical and theological reasons for the church's current practice of excluding women from ordination. Among the reasons given is the claim that, because of the need for *natural resemblance* in sacramental signs, only a male can fittingly represent the sacrificial aspect of Christ's saving love in the Eucharist, and thus only a male can be ordained. The Declaration also implies that "because the Incarnation of the Word took place according to the male sex . . ." then maleness is the primary sign or symbol of the plan of salvation in history.[22]

Understandably perhaps, the North American bishops cited did not engage in any lengthy discussion or commentary on the church's current position with respect to women and ordination. Many do, however, indicate that the question should remain open and that further study by theologians is necessary. In addition to recognizing the scriptural and theological study already devoted to the question over the last twenty years, the bishops could also begin acknowledging the roots of an alternate theological view on the fittingness of women to be a sign of the mystery of salvation. They themselves have proclaimed that women are created directly in the image of God, are indispensable signs of God's transcendence, and are essential to the sign value of the church as sacrament.

Surely a contradiction exists between the proclamation of such a profoundly biblical and theological view of women as *sign* and the current official theology and practice of the church which excludes women *a priori* as unfit signs for aspects of the mystery of salvation. One cannot have it both ways.

5. Practice in Rapport with Proclamation

The bishops have gone on record as advocating a number of practical action steps. Although the bishops alone are not responsible for the theological and structural change, nevertheless they must bear the major responsibility to implement this change. Discriminatory language, rites, laws, customs, financial prioritizing, and practices such as equal access to equal theological and pastoral education, just employment in parishes and schools, and women as teachers and spiritual directors in seminaries can only be changed by those who have and exercise the authority of pastoral office as it exists now.

Our North American bishops have begun to respond to the descriptive phase of feminist analysis and they have grasped as well certain aspects of the prescriptive phase, especially in their reflections that broaden theological reasoning and pastoral practice. But it is not a time for us to acquiesce; it is a time to *pester,* for the global transformation of consciousness regarding women has just begun. Linked with other liberation movements of our planet, such transformation is *the* call of our era.

Notes

1. For some idea of this knowledge explosion, see the bibliographies in: Jane Flax, "Postmodern and Gender Relations in Feminist Theory," *Signs* (Summer, 1987); Nancy Tuana, ed., *Newsletter on Feminism and Philosophy*, American Philosophical Association (April, 1988); Josephine Donovan, *Feminist Theory: The Intellectual Traditions of American Feminism* (New York: Ungar, 1985).

2. Flax, *ibid.* p. 622.

3. *Ibid.*, p. 623-26.

4. *Ibid.*, p. 623.

5. In recognition of this fact, the World Council of Churches has declared the next decade as a time of special world-wide concentration on the task of eradicating sexism and establishing in theory and practice the full dignity and equality of women in the churches and societies.

6. For some idea of the extent of this contribution, see the essays and bibliographies in: *Horizons* 14 (Fall, 1987); Joanne Wolski Conn, ed., *Women's Spirituality: Resources for Christian Development* (New York: Paulist, 1986); James Coriden, ed., *Sexism and Church Law: Equal Rights and Affirmative Action* (New York: Paulist, 1977). See also Mary Jo Weaver, *New Catholic Women: A Contemporary Challenge to Traditional Religious Authority* (New York: Harper and Row, 1985). For an excellent introductory essay describing Christian feminist liberation theology, see: Rosemary Radford Reuther, "Christian Quest for Redemptive Community," *Cross Currents* XXVII (Spring, 1988), 3-16.

7. I borrow the image of *pestering* from an article by Mary Jo Leddy, N.D.S., entitled, "Beyond Nagging: The Prophetic Role of Women in the Church" that appeared in the Canadian newspaper *Catholic New Times* (Toronto: November 6, 1988). Leddy reflects on the impact of the persistent Canaanite woman on the consciousness of Jesus and its consequences for widening his prophetic mission beyond his own people.

8. See, for example, Reuther's comments on this matter, *op cit.*

9. See, for instance, "Comments on the First Draft of the NCCB Pastoral Letter: Partners in the Mystery of Redemption," an evaluation issued by The Center of Concern (Washington, D.C.: June, 1988).

10. For a more thorough analysis of the Canadian bishops' texts, see: Mary Ellen Sheehan, I.H.M., "Recent Statements of Canadian Roman Catholic Bishops on Women in Church and Society: Toward a Reconstructed Theology and Practice," *Toronto Journal of Theology,* forthcoming. A similar analysis of the United States bishops' statements is underway by the same author.

11. As reported by Bishop Remi J. De Roo in "Women in the Church: Challenge for the Future," a Public Address given in Washington, D.C. October 12, 1986. Available on tape from Time Consultants, Washington, D.C.

12. George Cardinal Flahiff, "Address to the Synod of Bishops in Rome," October 14, 1980, *Origins 1* (1970-71), 295-296.

13. Bishop Robert Lebel, "Address to the Synod of Bishops in Rome," October 14, 1980, *Origins 10* (1980-81), 302.

14. Lebel, *op. cit.*

15. Bishop Bernard Hubert, *Complementing One Another, A Pastoral Letter on the Status of Women to the People of the Diocese of St-Jean-Longueuil,* December 7, 1984. English translation by Alexander Farrell and Antoinette Kinlough.

16. De Roo, *op. cit.*

17. On the Synodal process proposal, see: "Witness of Hope and Truth: Synodal Orientations." Intervention of Bishop Bernard Hubert, November 26, 1985, in *Twenty Years Later,* Canadian Conference of Catholic Bishops, Ottawa, 1986.

18. Archbishop James M. Hayes, "Address to the Synod of Bishops," October 9, 1987, *Origins 17* (1987-1988), 343-44.

19. Archbishop Raymond G. Hunthausen, *Pastoral Statement on Women,* April 30, Archdiocese of Seattle, Washington.

20. Bishop Victor Balke and Bishop Raymond Lucker, "Male and Female God Created Them," *Origins 11* (1981-1982), 333-38.

21. On this point, see Marie Gratton-Boucher's analysis of sexism and power in the church, "Power in the church: Must it Remain a Clerical Fiefdom?", translated by Robert Chodos, *Compass* (Spring, 1987), 517-31.

22. "Declaration on the Admission of Women to the Ministerial Priesthood," *Origins 6* (1976-1977), 517-31.

6

Two Views of the Church: The United States and the Vatican

Richard P. McBrien
University of Notre Dame

This paper is an exercise in comparative ecclesiology—comparing the ecclesiology of most U.S. Catholic theologians and pastoral ministers, including many bishops, on the one hand, and the ecclesiology of the principal centers of power in the Vatican, especially of Cardinal Joseph Ratzinger, on the other hand.

The Ecclesiology of the Catholic Church in the U.S.A.

The ecclesiology of most U.S. Catholic theologians and pastoral ministers including many bishops, tends to reflect the ecclesiology of Vatican II. Their primary ecclesial model, as was the Council's, is People of God.

For them, the Church is a people, a community of disciples on pilgrimage through history. The institutional, organizational and bureaucratic elements of the Church are necessary but subordinate to its life and mission. For this group of Catholics, persons always supersede the system, and pastoral needs always supersede regulations. Notice what I'm saying: I'm not saying that for those of us who operate out of this understanding regulations don't count and rules don't count. In a conflict situation, however, where the needs of people are at issue, we don't spite the needs of the person in order to remain faithful to the rule. Law in the Catholic Church is in the Roman law tradition, not in the Anglo-Saxon law tradition. The Roman law tradition is that the law is an ideal; in the Anglo-Saxon law tradition a law is a rule that has to be obeyed. I'll give you an example: you come to a stop sign at a four-way crossing in the middle of Utah and there's not a car, horse or truck in sight. The Roman law tradition is that you drive through it; why stop? The Anglo-Saxon tradition is that you come to a full stop, look both ways and then drive through.

To help bring out this approach to law I can remember an incident that occurred while I was studying in Rome. Many Americans—especially many conservative Americans—think this is not the right approach to law; but it is the approach that the popes and the Roman Curia have always adopted until it became somewhat less Italian. Many of my colleagues in Rome were studying canon law during the Council. Earlier in the decade Pope John XXIII issued a decree, *Veterum Sapientiae*, which insisted that all the ecclesiastical sciences would hereafter be taught in Latin. The American students who were over in Rome working on their canon law degrees were sitting in class as one of their professors came in and bravely read this new decree and said that because of the order of the Holy Father all dissertations would have to be written in Latin. You can imagine the terror in the hearts of Americans, especially, who already had enough trouble doing a dissertation in English. After the professor laid the whole thing out, he took off his glasses and said, "And of course, if you can't do it, you can't do it!" And the students began applauding and pounding their feet.

Yet people who don't understand the difference between the Roman and the Anglo-Saxon approach to law can look at that and say that is an offensive attitude toward the law; they have really insulted the Holy Father who intended this to be done. A Benedictine abbot went to see the pope; he presented a similar problem. He said, "Some of the people in our order tell me that they're unable to put this new decree into effect because they—the professors—do not use Latin well and their students would never understand them." Pope John replied: "If you can't do it, you can't do it."

The people of God tend to operate that way as well. It's not because we have a disrespect for the law or the regulations. Like Jesus, however, persons come before the rules. You obey the rules when the rules do in fact make it possible to enhance our being together as disciples of Jesus Christ. Ordinarily we expect rules and regulations—the system, if you will—to frame and support our life and our work as Christians. But when rules and regulations get in the way, to follow them to the letter would actually subvert our life as Christians and our mission.

There is a People-of-God ecclesiology, therefore, that is rooted in Scripture and in the post-biblical theological and doctrinal traditions of the Church, and is additionally rooted in actual pastoral experience.

Catholics who work out of this strongly pastoral ecclesiology rarely look first to the ecclesiastical rule-book before acting on a pastoral problem. They deal immediately with persons. On the basis of the cardinal virtue of prudence, they consult other persons of recognized wisdom and experience. They reflect and they pray. And even if they also consult the rule-books, their pastoral decisions are never based exclusively on them. Their model, whether they realize it or not, is Peter, the Church's "first pope," who broke all the rules to baptize the pagan centurion Cornelius and his entire household (Acts 10). No circumcision. No Jewish dietary regulations. And he ate with them besides, thereby committing the heinous sin of intercommunion! It was enough for Peter that the presence of the Holy Spirit was evident in Cornelius and his family. In other words, when he was actually challenged to justify baptizing Cornelius and his household and also eating with pagans without imposing upon them circumcision and Jewish dietary regulations, he said, "It was obvious the Spirit was there." See how far you get with an explanation like *that* today. There was no rule, there was no regulation Peter pointed to. He didn't even say, "I'm the first pope and I can do anything I want." His judgment was that this was a pastoral situation. To say that the Holy Spirit was there is simply another way of saying "It seemed right; it seemed to correspond with everything we know about God." That's what we really mean when we say that.

Can you imagine Jesus refusing to celebrate the eucharist with people because they happen to be gay? It's absurd when you put it that way, isn't it? And Jesus was accused precisely because he consorted with prostitutes—not commercially—who were in his company. He ate with tax-collectors and publicans. He was always in bad company, which is why he was crucified. He was a terrible threat, not so much to the Roman establishment as to the religious establishment. He was putting the whole religion business on its head. Religion was predicated on the assumption that religion was a matter of keeping the rules, and the rule-keepers—the people who wrote and enforced the rules—were the most important people; they got the best seats in the house. They were rewarded with the finest clothes with all of the insignia of office. And, of course, that was putting them out of business. If being religious doesn't mean necessarily following the rules, then the rule-keepers and the rule-writers are no longer the most important people.

I'm just saying here that those who work out of a People-of-God ecclesiology have, among other models, Peter, the so-called first pope, who was confronted with the first major pastoral crisis in the history of the Church: what do we do about non-Jews who want to become members of the community of disciples?

What do you do about that? That was the first real pastoral problem. Do they have to be circumcised? Do they have to eat from the same menu as we? There were some in the community who said Yes, that to join the company was to become Jewish. That doesn't make sense, especially since there is resistance: they don't want to become Jewish. And Peter made the same kind of decision in the face of that larger decision that he had made in the case of Cornelius. He said, "It doesn't seem right for these people to be held to circumcision and to the dietary law; here are people who want to follow Jesus, here are people who want to join with us and follow the way. Keep them out because they don't want to have some anatomical adjustment made? Keep them out simply because they have a preference for pork and bacon?" It didn't make sense to Peter and Barnabas and Saul and the rest.

That was the first major pastoral crisis in the Church which created the need for the first assembly—not an ecumenical council in the strict sense of the word—of Christians, the so-called council of Jerusalem, in the year of about forty-nine or fifty, where this whole issue had to be argued out. Peter argued the case on behalf of the others and his argument prevailed, not because he was the first pope. In fact, he wasn't even presiding at the council of Jerusalem, James was. Peter's opposition came from the traditionalists of his day, the so-called circumcision party, the "Judaizers." They're the ones who wrote the letters to report on Peter; it's a time-honored tradition. That's why they had to have a council, because of all the complaints that were coming in because Paul and Barnabas were bringing in all these Gentiles and not requiring circumcision: how can they do that? how can they get away with that? It's an irony not to be lost: it was the Church's first traditionalists who questioned the orthodoxy of the Church's first pope. We've come full circle now with Archbishop Marcel Lefebvre.

If the People-of-God image is the dominant ecclesial model for theologically and pastorally active Catholics in the United States, it is not the only one, though I have spent a lot of time on the People-of-God ecclesiology. Over against a People-of-God ecclesiology is a *communio* ecclesiology, which is the dominant Vatican ecclesiology. I will explain the contrast in due course. Furthermore, for the People-of-God ecclesiologists, as for the council, the Church is also a sacrament. Like any sacrament, the Church causes grace by signifying it. What is not signified is not caused. Consequently, the Church must always practice what it preaches. It must be a credible sign of what it is in reality; if it's not an effective sign of what it is, then it cannot effectively cause the grace of salvation that it embodies and communicates, namely, the corporate presence of Jesus Christ.

In this ecclesiology, prevalent here in the United States, besides being 1) People of God and 2) sacrament, the Church is, thirdly, a servant. In the words of the Third International Synod of Bishops of 1971, the Church's mission essentially includes the pursuit of justice and the transformation of the earth (para. 6). The Church, like Jesus himself, is in service of the kingdom, or reign, of God, and that kingdom, or reign, is one of justice and peace as well as of holiness and grace, to use the words of the Council's *Pastoral Constitution on the Church in the Modern World* (n. 39).

For these theologically and pastorally active Catholics, it is this document, *Gaudium et Spes,* that serves as the prism through which they view the whole reality of the Church. *Gaudium et Spes* speaks of a Church *in* the world in the *service* of the world. It is a pastorally oriented document; in fact, it is, in an unprecedented fashion, a pastorally composed document—the first in the history of the Church. Indeed, it is officially called a *Pastoral* Constitution, which explains why pastorally active Catholics have been drawn to it.

The Church of *Gaudium et Spes* doesn't turn only, and certainly not first, to the hierarchical magisterium to determine what it is that God is calling us to be and to do. There is a mentality that says when you want to know what you should do, when you want to know what God wants you to do, your first instinct is to check to see what the magisterium says. What are the teachings on this matter? What is the policy? What are the disciplinary regulations? I'm not saying we should ignore that, on the contrary. But *Gaudium et Spes* is a pastoral document, and it goes about it the way ordinary people go about it in pastoral situations. Your first instinct isn't to wonder where is the rule book. The first instinct is: what's the situation; what is the problem? And what does so and so say about it, I respect her judgment. Then you find out more about the situation. Then you make a judgment about what seems right.

Now, if there is a conflict and someone else is saying you can't do that because the rule says this, then you try to work out the conflict. In most situations, either the rule-book doesn't even cover the situation, or you find out that the decision you made pastorally is quite consistent with what the rule-book allows. *Gaudium et Spes* is not a document that says in order to understand what it means to be Church, you have to first of all go about being concerned about being faithful to the dictates of the hierarchical magisterium. Rather, it says you must first read the signs of the times. We have to see what God is actually up to; and you don't find what God is up to by reading the church papers or by reading official compilations of doctrine or by reading magazines called *The Pope Speaks*. You find out what God is up to by actually looking, listening, by being silent long enough to sense what is going on and, out of the virtue of prudence, by consulting other people for whom you have great respect. Out of that process you begin to conclude that God is up to something, God is calling us to move into this new area of missionary responsibility, or what have you. The Church of *Gaudium et Spes* first reads "the signs of the times" and tries to interpret them in the light of the gospel—with the subsequent guidance of the magisterium, to be sure.

Gaudium et Spes sees the world not as something racing headlong into sin and perdition, but as an historical reality, enlivened by the presence of the Spirit. The world is in process toward its final destiny, the kingdom, or reign, of God, when all the fruits of our human endeavor will be transformed and brought to their full flowering.

In addition to People of God, sacrament, and servant, the ecclesiology of these theologically and pastorally active U.S. Catholics is, fourthly, ecumenical. For them, as for the council, the Church is more than the Catholic Church. The Church includes Catholics and Protestant, Anglicans and Orthodox, and Oriental Christians of various kinds.

Their ecclesiology is, fifthly, collegial. The Church is universal, to be sure, but it is local as well. Indeed, the universal Church is a college of local churches. The Church is present wherever the Word of God is proclaimed and the sacraments are celebrated, whether these occur in a parish, a diocese, a national grouping of dioceses, or in a smaller, so-called "base community."

Sixthly and finally, the ecclesiology of the theologically and pastorally active Catholics in the Unites States is eschatological. They wouldn't be caught dead using that word "eschatological," and you won't hear that except in a meeting like this. You won't hear it in the pulpit—I hope. But "eschatology" and "eschaton" are theological terms of great importance; we have to translate them, that's all. The word "eschatology" comes from the Greek word "eschaton" that means "the last thing"—and the last thing is the fullness of the kingdom, the final outpouring of God's presence. To say that the Church is eschatological simply means that it is moving toward something beyond history, towards the final outpouring of God's presence. That means that the Church is not an end in itself but is simply a sign, an arrow shot out into the world pointing the way to this final out-pouring of God's presence.

In the meantime the Church offers itself, as *Lumen Gentium* says (art. 5), as the initial budding forth, you might say the initial explosion of God's presence. It strives always, therefore, to become more tomorrow than what it already is today. Because it is an eschatological community the Church is always subordinate to and must always be critiqued by the kingdom, or reign, of God.

Jesus said, in Matthew 7:21, "It is not the one who says Lord, Lord, who comes into the kingdom, but the one who does the will of the Father." Now it's obviously better to do the will of God *and* say Lord, Lord. But if you have to make a choice, then it's better to do the will of God and not say "Lord, Lord," than to say "Lord, Lord" and not do the will of God. St. Augustine made that point, and Karl Rahner used it to great effect in one of his writings: "Many whom God has, the Church does not have; and many whom the Church has, God does not have." Which is simply another way of saying that although the Church and the kingdom overlap, they are not the same. It's possible to be doing God's will, to be within the orbit of God's kingdom, and not to be in the Church, not to be among those who say "Lord, Lord"; just as it is possible to be in the Church saying "Lord, Lord" until you become hoarse, but not living according to the principles of the Lord himself.

What holds all these ecclesiological things together for theologically and pastorally active Catholics in the United States is the primary biblical and conciliar image of the People of God. The church is people: we are the Church. That's why liberals, progressives, moderates—call them what you will—have got to be very careful in their use of language. Sometimes people can get very discouraged and even annoyed and even angry and tempted to be done with it all and leave the Church. Sometimes we assimi-late the language—if I may say—of the oppressor and accept the oppressor's ecclesiology and make a decision on the basis of the oppressor's ecclesiology. We allow the oppressor to define the terms. Leaving the Church does not mean turning one's back on the hierarchy or slamming the chancery door. Leaving the Church means deciding not to go back to Thanksgiving dinner with the family. It means deciding not to have dinner any longer with the people that up until now you have called family.

That's why the decision is far more difficult, when understood properly, than the mere decision to say I'm going to have nothing more to do with this pope or these bishops. That's easy. To leave the Church really means to say I no longer want to be part of that table fellowship. I no longer want to be invited, nor will I accept an invitation. That's a different thing. And the reason we can say that is because the Church is people. It's not just an institution; institutional arrangements are such items—someone has to set the date for Thanksgiving Day. Who could calculate Easter on their own? The institutional arrangement makes possible the really important stuff.

The Ecclesiology of the Vatican

If it is both accurate and fair to suggest that Cardinal Ratzinger's ecclesiology is representative of the present Vatican administration (and notice I said the *present* Vatican administration, because Vatican administrations come and go), then one can legitimately conclude that the Vatican's current view of the Church is more faithfully reflected in *Lumen Gentium*, chapter 3, than in *Gaudium et Spes. Lumen Gentium,* chapter three, speaks to the hierarchical structure of the Church. I think it really is possible and fair to make this point of comparison, because I think there are people in the Church today for whom *Lumen Gentium,* chapter three, is the most important section of the Council documents. In fact, many very conservative Catholics often quote *Lumen Gentium* 25, about our obligation to accept "merely authentic teachings." But contrast *Lumen Gentium,* chapter three with *Gaudium et Spes,* which is not concerned primarily with the structure of the Church, but primarily with the reality of the Church in the world, in the service of the world. Very different perspectives. Note, however, that *Lumen Gentium* 3 does not contradict *Gaudium et Spes* nor *vice versa.* It's like teaching software to a computer: it's got the same hardware, but you select your software, and you can only get so much out of one kind of software while another piece of software does something else. Continuing that analogy, *Gaudium et Spes* software incorporates *Lumen Gentium* 3 and puts it in proper context. I think, however, that

Lumen Gentium 3 software doesn't necessarily incorporate *Gaudium et Spes.*

The wider context of Cardinal Ratzinger's understanding and interpretation of *Lumen Gentium* is his view of the Church as primarily a mystery and a *communio*, i.e., a reality imbued with the hidden presence of God and a communion in the life of the Trinity. But mystery and *communio*, like almost every other major element in Christian theology, are two-sided and two-dimensional: both natural and supernatural, both human and divine, both historical and eternal.

The tendency in Cardinal Ratzinger's—and the Vatican's—view of the Church is to reduce the both/and relationship to an either/or relationship, to set the natural against the supernatural, the human against the divine, the historical against the eternal. The supernatural tends to suppress the natural, the divine tends to suppress the human, and the eternal tends to suppress the historically contingent. Let me show you how the Cardinal brings this out even in public addresses.

In the summer of 1988, in a remarkably polemical speech to the bishops of Chile soon after his efforts to placate Archbishop Marcel Lefebvre came to ruin, Cardinal Ratzinger directly attacked what he regards as the major deficiencies of the post-Vatican II Church: namely, liturgical reforms that dilute the sacred element of the Mass, turning it into "interesting entertainment." He castigated theological views that regard Vatican II teachings as a "superdogma" erasing previous Church tradition; and a watering down of Catholic belief, in ecumenical and missionary activities, in an effort to avoid the appearance of claiming sole proprietorship of full divine revelation and the right to judge humanity.

Cardinal Ratzinger's remarks on liturgy were especially revealing. "The liturgy is reduced . . . to language and gestures of ordinary life such as greeting and common signs of friendship," he complained. "The liturgy is not a festival, nor a pleasant gathering." And what would Ratzinger say of pastors who are liturgically inept? He says, "it is unimportant, even in the remotest way, that the pastor proceeds in generating evocative ideas or imaginative trappings. The greatness of the liturgy is not based on a person offering an interesting entertainment." Is one to conclude from Cardinal Ratzinger's remarks that the Eucharist is truly liturgical only when it is unpleasant, unfriendly, unimaginative, and uninteresting, because then we know that it's truly mysterious? If it's that mysterious, why would anyone want to come?

Cardinal Ratzinger suggested to the bishops of Chile that there is some legitimacy to Archbishop Lefebvre's complaints. There have been so many abuses since Vatican II, the Cardinal insisted, that we should make the Lefebvre schism "an occasion for an examination of conscience" so that the abuses may be corrected. Cardinal Ratzinger has perhaps forgotten or deliberately ignored the fact that Archbishop Lefebvre opposed the Council *at* the Council. Lefebvre's negative attitude and behavior toward the Council had nothing to do with what happened *after* the Council. He was one of the major opponents of Vatican II at Vatican II, and Ratzinger or anyone else who suggests that the reason why the Lefebvre movement has taken root is because of abuses of Vatican II either doesn't know history or is deliberately denying it or trying to rewrite it. Archbishop Marcel Lefebvre was one of the most vigorous, vehement opponents of Vatican II *at* the Council.

In any case, how might the Church "correct" the "abuses" to which Cardinal Ratzinger referred? Included in this Vatican view of the Church is an inherent justification of the use of bureaucratic mechanisms of enforcement. In one of the standard Latin manuals of theology, the so-called Spanish *Summa*, the Church was defined as a "perfect society with full legislative, judicial and coercive power." That's one of the principal theses, or propositions, of one of the best of the Latin manuals from the pre-Vatican II period. If the Church is a perfect society, more divine than human, more eternal than historical, it must have the institutional wherewithal to preserve its identity and to defend itself against substantial corruption from within or from without. This is an integral part of Vatican ecclesiology today, just as it was an integral part of Vatican ecclesiology before the council.

The Church, however, is a community of disciples, a community that comes about out of conversion and not out of compulsion. In other words, no one is forced to be a member of the Church. One is in the Church because one wants to be in the Church; one wants to be a part of the company of Jesus Christ because one is captivated by the person of Jesus Christ and believes in Jesus Christ as the Lord of history and is prompted by the Holy Spirit to make that testimony of faith and to follow Jesus in the way. The very notion of *punishing* people who, out of the same freedom, decide to do something else is so contrary to the whole thing. Moral persuasion, for sure. Example, for sure. But punishment? Thumb screws and racks? We've had those in our history; today the methods perhaps are more sophisticated, more subtle. Nevertheless, punishment contradicts the very notion of the Church as a voluntary community. The only way that we can bring around a recalcitrant member is by moral persuasion and by example, with patience and kindness and love; if that fails, there is no other recourse. The Ratzinger-Curial mentality is that if that fails, then you've got to do something really serious.

In one of the most celebrated debates at the council, on November 8, 1963, mid-way through the second session, Cardinal Joseph Frings, of Cologne, West Germany, clashed with Cardinal Alfredo Ottaviani, Cardinal Ratzinger's predecessor as head of what was then known as the Holy Office.

Cardinal Frings charged that the "procedures [of the Holy Office] are out of harmony with modern times, are a source of harm to the faithful and of scandal to those outside the Church. No Roman congregation," he continued, "should have authority to accuse, judge and condemn an individual who has had no opportunity to defend himself. With all due reverence and gratitude for the devoted individuals who spend their lives in the difficult work of the Holy Office, we feel that its methods should be basically revised." Certainly this was one of the most dramatic moments in the history of the Second Vatican Council. A cardinal from West Germany, one of the leaders of the Council, told it straight out: you've got to do something about this congregation: you've got a lot of abuses, and it's a scandal!

Cardinal Ottaviani's reaction was swift and sharp. He protested "most vigorously" the condemnation levelled by Cardinal Frings. "It should not be forgotten," Ottaviani declared, "that the prefect of the Holy Office is none other than the sovereign pontiff himself . . . . All decisions of the Holy Office are approved by the Pope personally, and thus such criticisms are a reflection on the Vicar of Christ."

Cardinal Ottaviani then repeated his criticism of the doctrine of collegiality still under debate at the council: "Those who propose the collegiality of the bishops proceed in a vicious circle since they presume that the Apostles existed and acted as a collegial body . . . . The fact is that only Peter has responsibility for the whole flock of Christ. It is not the sheep who lead Peter, but it is Peter who leads the sheep."

Cardinal Ottaviani's ecclesiology and the methods of his Holy Office have been carried forward in some measure in the far more sophisticated ecclesiology of Cardinal Ratzinger and in the less blatantly severe methods of his Congregation for the Doctrine of the Faith. The battle that raged on

November 8, 1963, and throughout the Council between Cardinal Frings and the majority of the Council Fathers, on the one hand, and Cardinal Ottaviani and the minority of Council Fathers, on the other—that battle continues in the Church today.

Those who were defeated at the council some 25 years ago and their successors continue to fight on behalf of their view of the Church today. No problem with that; they have a right to do that. What they lost in open debate in the council hall they now seek to win back by bureaucratic force. To that they do not have a right. People have a right to say, "I still don't see it; I still don't agree. It still bothers me that . . ., etc., etc." That is fine. We're all brothers and sisters who should feel free to challenge and question. But if we have a fight that is "in the family," it ought to be among family members, and it ought to be done in the open. And what is lost? We already had this argument played out in the Second Vatican Council, in the world wide meeting of all the bishops of the Catholic Church. When all of those arguments were voiced, when the final votes were taken, the Council came down on the side of ecumenism, collegiality, People of God, servanthood and all the rest. The Ottaviani forces lost. It doesn't mean they don't have a right to continue to say they are unhappy with that. They would like still to press their case. Fine. But do it fairly, do it openly. Don't use the mechanisms of the bureaucracy in order to negate what was freely and fairly and openly decided upon, by the family, the last time we had a family get-together.

The Ratzinger predecessors opposed collegiality at the council; they oppose collegiality today. They opposed a People-of-God understanding of the Church at the council; they oppose it still today, preferring instead the language of mystery and *communio*—anything to extract the Church from the grubbiness and contingencies of peoplehood and of human history.

The defeated minority's ecclesiology is evident again in the recent Vatican draft document on episcopal conferences, *Instrumentum Laboris* ("The Theological and Juridical Status of Episcopal Conferences").

In the interest of saving time I will just recapitulate some of the remaining material in my paper. (See Note 1.) I will simply present a summary of some of the problems with the draft document on the national episcopal conferences. Let me put it in terms which are less theological and more political, to understand what the fight is all about.

If you in fact hold to a highly centralized, indeed monarchical, understanding of authority in the Church, then national episcopal conferences get in the way. If the Chief Executive Officer and his cabinet have to work with a union—that's what a national episcopal conference is, analogously—then it's a lot harder to discipline and to mandate policy. The preference is for a benign factory owner, who comes in and makes private deals with individuals. It's too bad for the rest; you can either abide by the contract or quit. You won't get a better job somewhere else because if the other factory owners are the same way you're caught in a network of injustice. From this centralized point of view national episcopal conferences obviously diminish the capacity of the Chief Executive Officer and his cabinet from exercising authority in the Church, because you have to deal with the human.

National episcopal conferences are also unpopular with certain kinds of bishops who in their dioceses want to operate in that same kind of unhindered, unimpeded way of exercising authority. What happens, politically, is that you have a trade-off: the central headquarters, in other words, secures its own power base by going out and getting the support of people—key voters, if you will, key members of the senate or the house or whatever it might be—in return for favors. That's life, that's politics.

The same thing happens in the Church. In return for opposing national episcopal conferences, for opposing the human, certain archbishops are allowed to function as king of the hill in their own dioceses. And they don't have to work through Rome, either. If a bishop decides that women are not going to be allowed to function as lectors or eucharistic ministers, as long as he's got his lines cleared with the Vatican, he can do whatever he wants. But if he does it and the union has already got an agreement that we will not do things this way, then you're going to hear from people, including brother bishops. It's not only the fellow over there across the Atlantic that you have to keep happy at Christmas time. There might be someone up the Interstate or across the river who is also going to be looking over your shoulder.

Most people say that's a good thing because in union there is strength; after all, we're social beings, we applaud Solidarity in Poland because it's safely many thousand miles away. But as a matter of fact, the same principle should apply in the Church. So national episcopal conferences are simply ways of institutionalizing the solidarity, the commonality, of the churches. The Church is not just a collection of individual, self-contained, isolated units whose only unity is their linkage with the central office. Rather the Church itself is a community or college of local communities, each of which in itself is the Church, the Body of Christ, but each of which is in communion with all the other local churches, and together they constitute the Church universal. That's what the fight over national episcopal conferences is all about.

I have good news to report if you haven't been following the news. By a vote of two-thirds plus two the U.S. Catholic bishops at their November, 1988, meeting in Washington did decide to send in a negative report saying that this document on National Episcopal Conferences can't even be fixed and should be re-written. That's where we stand on it. So the bishops themselves have acknowledged that the document is radically flawed, but it's radically flawed because the document is an effort on the part of those who wrote it to restore the ecclesiology of the pre-Vatican II period, which is an uncollegial ecclesiology. The Vaticanists want to restore the old-fashioned, centralized, notion of the Church. And unions get in the way of this, because unions, like the national episcopal conferences, place another layer of real authority between the central headquarters and the local church. That's why these documents are filled with references to the importance of the local bishops and trying to protect the integrity of the local bishop.

I have a concluding word: the bishops' action is consistent with the ecclesiology that I've been talking about on the U.S. side. The Church is not either universal or local; it is both universal and local. The unique Petrine ministry of the bishop of Rome must be exercised and honored, but that ministry cannot suppress or unduly subordinate the role of the local churches in their individual, regional, national and patriarchal groupings.

If I can make a play off of Peter Chirico's paper given earlier at this symposium: just as the bishop of Rome's teaching authority is not unlimited, neither is the bishop of Rome's jurisdictional authority unlimited. The principle of subsidiarity is central to the most representative view of the Church in the United States. Nothing should be done by a higher agency that could be done as well if not better by a lower agency. Decisions, in other words, are to be made at the point closest to where they will have their primary, immediate impact, and those decisions are to be shaped in largest measure by the religious experience and pastoral needs of those who are closest to the scene. In other words, decisions which affect the Church ought to be made by the Church, and the people—all of the people—are the Church. If participation is an American value, it is also a Catholic value: we are the people of God.

One final comment. The whole discussion that this exercise in comparative ecclesiology opens up does have some very practical, pastoral implications. After all, despite what I said, you can still say to yourself, and I think legitimately so, well, even this whole debate over national episcopal conferences, how does it affect me in the parish? How does it affect me in the diocese?

This conflict of ecclesiologies has to be seen in the context of what's going on in the life of the Church, beyond theology but as a reflection of theology. For example, look at the pattern of appointments—there have been significant changes in the American hierarchy, and it's not unplanned. (See Note 2.) Cardinal Edmund Szoka replaced Cardinal Dearden in Detroit. That wasn't because it was time for a Polish background bishop. There are plenty of very open-minded, progressive, pastorally sensitive and credible Polish priests in Detroit who would have been welcomed by the priests and people of Detroit. John O'Connor going to New York, Bernard Law going to Boston, Frank Stafford going to Denver, Roger Mahoney going from Stockton to Los Angeles. Most people, even well informed people, don't follow that.

Can I take an example that comes close to home in Washington? I notice you just reelected Slade Gorton to the Senate (1988). Remember when he was defeated. I know you probably had some local issues regarding energy or Boeing. But as I followed the Gorton Senate race when he was defeated by Brock Adams, one of the things that came back to haunt him was his vote in support of Manion (and he should have voted against him, because Manion is from South Bend and we know Manion: he makes Dan Quayle look like Judge Brandeis). Slade Gorton's vote for Manion was a politically damaging vote because it was obviously a political trade-off. Nothing wrong with trade-offs. But his vote really did him in with a lot of Washington state voters. Now the Manion vote was not an isolated vote. When Ed Meese was the Attorney General, he wanted people like Manion in the Federal Court. He didn't care whether they were qualified jurists. He didn't care whether other jurists, other lawyers, other judges, would respect him; he was concerned with the ideological dimension. It was a litmus test. I take a great risk that this will sound cynical, but I think the best way to understand what is going on in the Church is to see the parallel with the political realm. There's nothing bad about that. Imagine Ed Meese in the Catholic Church, with no Senate to check him, making all the decisions on major episcopal appointments—archbishop appointments in particular—picking people, not because they are great jurists or, in this case, because they are great pastoral leaders, people that the priests and people of their diocese would spontaneously accept. But rather picking people whom we know are really going to toe the line, that we can count on when this issue and that issue come up—law and order, crime, divorce—and that's the only thing we care about. That's the only possible justification for the Manion appointment.

Imagine that taking place in the Catholic Church, but taking place without a U.S. Senate to check, to hold hearings, as they did in the Bork hearings or the Ginsburg hearings for the Supreme Court. That's what is going on in the Catholic Church. A lot of people are going to wake up someday. All that you in the Seattle church have gone through is *not* typical. A lot of people, in other dioceses, are going to wake up someday and realize that the things they just took for granted they can't do anymore because of the major shift in bishops and a new restoration mentality.

Now, in the short run, as long as they have a pastor who comes out of that generation which developed pastoral credibility and has pastoral experience and pastoral realism, as Peter had, they'll be able to do what the Catholics of Chicago did in the last years of Cardinal Cody. Chicago Catholics remained Catholic in spite of Cody, but Catholicism became a kind of congregationalist religion, a parish-centered religion. Then when the burden of Cardinal Cody was lifted and he was brought to the eternal Kingdom and when Cardinal Bernardin came, they were able to function once again as a fully diocesan church more consistent with the Catholic reality of Church. That has worked, but at the parish level, in the interim, the people of God have to work their way through this ideological bishop. They no longer have a bishop as a supporter and an empowerer, a facilitator and an encourager, a stimulator of missionary activity, but rather a barrier, a law-enforcement officer, a pain in the neck.

That approach will work. But what if things change at the parish level, and there are no longer pastors who work in a pastorally collaborative way, who are sensitive to the differences in the community, rich and poor, black and white, male and female and all the rest that that implies? What happens if you find, because of changes in the vocations situation, that the people also at the parish level are highly clericalized in their mentality and have psychological orientations, not just deadened, but even worse, sexually neuter. Parishes may be led by men with no real sense of their sexual identity, who therefore will find it very difficult to relate to anybody in any kind of profound and mature way. What happens then?

Well, it's already happening, and so people then are going to go shopping around parishes. As long as there is a parish community with pastoral leadership that's relatively nearby, people can make that choice. Some people don't make that choice. We're losing people, not because they have decided they don't believe any longer, but because it's just too inconvenient to continue to be a part of a particular community of worship.

What happens when there aren't any nearby parishes, when the only priests around are priests that you don't want to hear, that you cannot interact with because of their pastoral mentality? That's why this issue is very serious. It is not that we should not have hope. On the contrary, one has to really believe in the Holy Spirit's presence in the Church, and one has to really sense the presence of so many people who in spite of all this continue to function in the Church as effective pastoral and ministerial leaders. We may therefore be moving to the time—and who says this is bad?—when because of the vocations crisis at the priestly level and because of the appointments pattern at the episcopal level, we will have the reemergence of lay leadership in the Church. Perhaps this is what God is bringing us to help us to move along to the state where we really are the Church as the people of God without any inflexible clergy/laity lines.

On the other hand, we've got to be concerned about these developments because we're not simply a congregational church with a Baptist-style polity. There is an important and indeed irreplaceable role for bishops and the bishop of Rome, Peter's successor. The Church needs their ministry at every level—diocesan, regional, national and universal. John XXIII was, after all, an extraordinary gift to the universal Church. Paul Hallinan was a special gift to the church of Atlanta. Albert Meyer was an exceptional gift to the church of Chicago. And John Dearden was a precious gift to the church of Detroit. Raymond Hunthausen is still, in my opinion, an exceptional gift to the church of Seattle.

Our hope and our prayer is for some healing of the conflict between these two views of the Church. It would help a lot if the next several episcopal openings were filled by men with the pastoral aptitude of a Rembert Weakland, a Raymond Hunthausen, or indeed of a John Dearden. And it might help even more if, sometime in the 21st century at whose threshold we all stand, such appointments were drawn not only from those with names like Rembert, Raymond, and John, but also with names like Esther, Judith, and Ruth.

Note One:
American Bishops' Critique of the Draft on
Episcopal Conferences

I think the best way to see what is going on in the Church is to see the parallel with the political world.

The draft document, written not only in the spirit but also in the letter of Cardinal Ratzinger's own *Ratzinger Report* and other of his writings, rejects the collegial nature of national episcopal conferences as well as their teaching authority, or *manus magisterii*. According to the document, only when the bishops act as a body with the pope do we have a true *actio collegialis*. When bishops act together regionally or nationally, that action is collegial only in an "analogical, theologically improper" way (II.2). Astonishingly, the document even proposes that episcopal conferences are only a little more than 100 years old.

The Vatican draft document takes care to defend the individual authority of each bishop against the incursions of an episcopal conference. "Sacramental consecration," the document asserts, "establishes a relationship between Christ and the individual bishop; by virtue of such a relationship he alone represents and makes present the Lord as head of his people" (III.1). Consequently, "the individual bishop by divine right has the duty and responsibility to decide and deliberate in the spiritual pastoral order all that which regards the good of his people" (IV.2).

The document sets the universality of the church over against its particularity, or its local character. For the Vatican, the Church is, "first of all, a single and universal-catholic reality" (IV.2.c). The clear implication is that local churches, at the diocesan, regional, and national levels, derive their ecclesial reality entirely from the universal Church, as if these local churches were simply administrative subdivisions of the universal Church. All ecclesiastical power, including teaching authority, therefore, resides ultimately in the pope and his Curia. Nothing really counts without papal and curial approbation.

In an address to his fellow bishops June, 1988, at St. John's University, Collegeville, Minnesota, John May, Archbishop of St. Louis and President of the National Conference of Catholic Bishops, criticized the Vatican draft document on three counts, and in so doing underscored the difference between the Vatican's view of the Church and that of theologically and pastorally active Catholics in the United States.

First, Archbishop May said, the Vatican document asserts that episcopal conferences are merely practical contrivances, without theological foundation. The document implies that the Church could do very well without them, in fact. Archbishop May challenged that view and cited *Lumen gentium,* article 23, in rebuttal: "It has come about through divine providence that, in the course of time, different churches set up in various places by the apostles and their successors joined together in a multiplicity of organically united groups." The council listed under such groupings, first, the ancient patriarchal churches and then episcopal conferences which it says are able to contribute to collegiality "in like manner" (*"simili rationi"*). The council's Decree on the Bishop's Pastoral Office in the Church makes a similar linkage between episcopal conferences and the ancient synods and local councils.

The Vatican draft document also asserts that episcopal conferences are only analogically collegial. Archbishop May, reflecting a different view of the Church, rejected the notion of an "individualistic, atomized" exercise of episcopal authority. Every bishop in his own diocese remains part of the college of bishops and, therefore, teaches and acts always within that collegial reality (see again *Lumen gentium,* n. 23). "If this is true of one bishop," Archbishop May observed, "it cannot then be less true of 300."

Thirdly, and finally, Archbishop May argued, even the new Code of Canon Law (canon 753) acknowledges the teaching authority of national episcopal conferences. Furthermore, these conferences have by now established a substantial record of corporate teaching. "I would note," he said at Collegeville, "that our episcopal conference has been making doctrinal pronouncements for at least 20 years." The pastoral letters on peace and the U.S. economy are two dramatic cases in point.

Archbishop May's speech to his fellow bishops provided a preview of the more formal response of the National Conference of Catholic Bishops, drafted by a committee of former presidents of the NCCB and approved by a vote of two-thirds plus two at the November, 1988, Washington meeting of the U.S. bishops.

The bishops criticize the confused and inconsistent manner in which key terms are used in the Vatican document: collegiality, *communio, manus magisterii,* dogmatic foundations, and divine institution. By way of example, let me quote the relevant paragraph on *communio:* "*Communio* provides a reliable central and governing concept for the document, but the interpretation given to it throughout is heavily individualistic and universalistic. Communion within and among particular churches is neglected, mentioned only once and in passing. Thus the argument in this text neglects the regional *communio* or *corpus ecclesiarum* which *Lumen Gentium* 23 ascribed to the workings of divine providence. There are in this document only the universal Church and the particular (diocesan) Church. Organic groupings of Church are not considered ecclesiologically relevant."

In an accompanying Background Paper the bishops summarize the nine major defects of the Vatican draft, and in so doing highlight the characteristic deficiencies of contemporary Vatican ecclesiology:

(1) It is very lacking in historical argument, whether with regard to precedents in the history of the Church for regional groupings of churches and of bishops or with regard to the textual histories of conciliar statements or canons of the new Code.

(2) It is quite selective in its appeals to Vatican II, leaving out of consideration important aspects of the conciliar teaching on communion, collegiality, and the role of the episcopal conferences.

(3) Vatican II is read as having settled issues which it deliberately left open, with the result that the draft adopts only one of the positions represented in the conciliar debates.

(4) The draft contains many simply apodictic statements, for which no theological or juridical evidence is adduced, so that they seem to be asserted as if they go without saying.

(5) No recognition is given that at Vatican II, in the course of the revision of the Code, and in the scholarly literature, other views have been proposed by serious and respected theologians and canonists.

(6) Theological and practical questions are confused, as if the latter inevitably have profound theological roots and with no consideration that they can be addressed by themselves without the need for an authoritative settling of disputed theological questions.

(7) The immense ecumenical significance of the topic is simply ignored, with little attention being given to the experience of synodality in the Eastern churches.

(8)   The draft shows evidence of hasty composition. It is at times internally inconsistent. Whole paragraphs appear to have been taken *verbatim* from published articles of various authors, some of them written before the Synod of 1985.

(9)   As a result of all this, the impression is given of a draft written in defence of an already known and established thesis rather than of a document which represents the results of the new, broader, and deeper study of the issues requested by the 1985 Synod of Bishops.

The major question which these criticisms raise is this: On what grounds is it assumed by the authors of the draft that what Vatican II and the new Code left open, *can* and *must* now be settled authoritatively?

The U.S. bishops' critique of the Vatican document accurately reflects the views of theologically and pastorally active Catholics in the United States.   For them the Church is not *either* universal *or* local; it is *both* universal *and* local. Of course, the unique Petrine ministry of the Bishop of Rome must be exercised and honored, but that ministry cannot suppress or unduly subordinate the local churches in their individual, regional, national, and patriarchal groupings.   The principle of subsidiarity is central to the most representative view of the Church in the United States: nothing should be done by a higher agency that can be done as well, if not better, by a lower agency.

Note Two:
The Politics of Ecclesial Appointments

This discussion of the two views of the Church—Vatican and American—would be largely academic if it were not for the fact that the Vatican appoints all the bishops and that almost all of the important bishops the Vatican has been appointing in these post-Jadot years (i.e., since 1980) have been of a particular ideological type. They accept without question the authority of the pope and his Curia as if uncritical acceptance of all papal and curial decisions were directly willed by the Lord himself, and as if the present papal-curial governmental structure were also directly willed by the Lord. Consequently, these appointees are at ease with a highly centralized, bureaucratic, and institutional model of the Church. They are at ease with the notion that they are, for all practical purposes, deputies, or vicars, of the pope, and that their dioceses are simply administrative subdivisions of the universal Church. In their view of the Church, each of them and each of their dioceses is related to the pope and the Holy See on a one-to-one basis. Larger groupings of dioceses and of bishops are no more than "practical contrivances."

7

Authority in the Twentieth Century: "Whose Image and Whose Inscription?" A Biblical Reflection

Karen Barta
Seattle University

The question in the title plays upon two biblical texts. Most immediately it evokes the story of Jesus' encounter with opponents who tried to get him into trouble with Roman authorities on the issue of Jews paying taxes to Rome. After demanding that they show him a coin, Jesus asked: "Whose image [*eikon*] and inscription is this?" They answered, "Caesar's."[1] If we reflected on our experience of authority in the Church and asked ourselves—"Whose image and inscription shaped this experience?"—what would we answer? Would we be able to say that our experience of Church authority reflects the profound mysteries of our faith? Could we say that it draws its vitality from the myths and metaphors, the images and inscriptions, of the Gospel? Or would we have to admit that our experience of authority within the Church all too often bears the business image and secular inscription of Caesar?

A second and much older biblical text echoes within Jesus' probing question. One of the very first lessons Sacred Scripture teaches is that we are all created in "the image [*eikon*] and likeness" of God.[2] This ancient belief is the touchstone for Jesus' command that we give to God what belongs to God. Giving to Caesar what belongs to Caesar means not giving away what belongs to God; it means keeping intact our own imaging of the Divine.

In a provocative study of authority in the modern world, Richard Sennett is especially alert to the images that support leadership styles.[3]

Authority, his study suggests, is very much in the eye of the beholder. In re-imaging authority within the Church, one might well begin by looking at the images underlying the dominant modes of authority in modern society. Accordingly, Part I of this paper outlines Sennett's insightful portrayal of the malignant forms of institutionalized authority, the fears they engender, and the need for a journey of transformance. Part II offers a biblical response. It suggests, by way of examples, how biblical stories and metaphors can help liberate our imaginations from the corrosive images of paternalism. Schooled in the gospel's symbolic reversals, the practice of authority within the Church can become a means for mutual empowerment.

Modern Images of Authority

Bonds of Rejection

According to Richard Sennett, the modern dilemma of authority, the peculiar fear it inspires, is born of our mixed emotions: feeling attracted to strong figures of authority and at the same time doubting their legitimacy. As a result, "we have become adept at building bonds of rejection with authorities. These bonds permit us to depend on those whom we fear. . . . The trouble is that these bonds also permit the authorities to use us: they can exercise control of a very basic sort over those who seem on the surface to be rebelling."[4]

Using case histories, Sennett identifies three ways of rejection that actually bind subjects to authorities. The first, *fantasized disappearance* is thinking that everything would be just fine if only the person in charge would disappear. "If only the pastor would leave." "If only this pope or that bishop weren't in office at this time." A second way of establishing rejection bonds with an authority involves *idealized substitution*. Here one uses an authority figure like a negative image from which to print the positive. "Father So-and-So is exactly the opposite of what a pastor should be!" A third method, *disobedient dependence*, requires purposely doing something against the will of an authority figure in order to prove one's independence. In fact, though, one is actually psychologically dependent upon the authority to react by showing strength. For when an authority images strength, it gives others a sense of security and power.

By strategies such as these, however, modern society shows itself responding to authority with fear and rejection. Yet the patterns of rejection we fall into, rather than effecting the desired change in authorities, actually succeed in binding us to them.

Authority as Paternalistic

The two dominant forms of authority in our time, Sennett argues, are paternalism and autonomy. Sennett traces the development of paternalism from patriarchy, which operates only in societies where the people are *conscious* of their blood relations. Patriarchy engenders patrimonialism which uses *property* as the means for passing on to one's male children power and influence in society. When it was no longer possible to guarantee one's male progeny power through ownership of property, paternalism developed as the primary means for keeping men in positions of authority through the *roles* they held in society as governor, judge, scholar, lawyer, doctor, bishop, priest. Historically, then, society moved from patriarchy to patrimonialism to paternalism.[5]

Sennett traces the emergence of paternalism to the era of high capitalism which borrowed the father image from a kinder, more stable time and superimposed it on the image of a boss. In the preceding centuries, most fathers were in fact the bosses of their children, on farms and in businesses run as family enterprises. But in the 19th century, "this paternalistic metaphor was frequently and widely used in the new economy, pasted over the stark material fact that bosses were anything but supportive, protective, loving leaders of their employers."[6]

The philosopher John Locke reasoned that destroying the material foundations of patrimonialism would curb the power of kings and result in a greater freedom for adults outside the family. But, Sennett argues, "what Locke and other liberal idealists did not anticipate is that *what could be materially destroyed could be imaginatively rebuilt:* metaphors linking fathers and bosses, father and leaders."[7]

The strength of the metaphor of father lies ultimately in what it fuses together, namely care and power. But paternalistic authority offers, in the end, a false love. False because the leader's care for those subject to him reaches only as far as his self-interest. Within paternalism one person actually determines the boundaries of reality for others. Paternalism seeks to enjoy the reality-control fathers have over their children. But paternalism lacks the constraints that exist within real families. "For," as Sennett notes, "ordinary fathers do not make such one-sided demands upon their children."[8] Fathers die; children grow up, leave home, and become parents themselves.

As illustration, Sennett recounts the case history of George Pullman, a leading industrialist of his day, who built Pullman, Illinois, as a model company town. When his employees went on strike in 1894, he lamented "I was like a father to them." In 1912, an analysis of the Pullmann strike by Jane Addams, a social worker, appeared under the title "A Modern Lear." She argued that both Pullman and King Lear tried to use their authority to control the boundaries of reality for other people. Against this controlled existence, both Pullman's employees and Lear's daughter Cordelia rebelled. Sennett concludes:

> It might be said of all these cases that the surrogates were bad fathers rather than false ones, but I think this is too tepid. There is a promise of nurturance made in paternalistic ideologies, and the essential quality of nurturance is denied: that one's care will make another grow stronger.[9]

In reality, those subject to paternalistic authority do not grow stronger.

Authority as Autonomous

According to Sennett, the other form of authority prevalent in modern society is autonomy. If paternalism offers a false love, autonomy recognizes no love for those it governs. Autonomy as a form of authority is expedient. It gets things done because it has the skills, the expertise, or the character required for the task. It exercises authority without requiring support from outside. Autonomous authority is perceived as strong enough to act on its own, independently, without deference to the desires of others. Those who take this approach are generally known for their self-discipline and the freedom with which they seem to act. This is the pastor or administrator who consults the parish after decisions are made, encourages only superficial participation in the parish's liturgical life, and runs all the parish meetings (whether he's there or not).

Autonomy as a way of exercising authority is attractive because many people associate autonomy with freedom. The American ideals of freedom and individualism especially play into this form of power. Yet what holds a community together are compassion, trust, and reassurance. Thus Sennett concludes: "The dominant forms of authority in our lives are destructive; they lack nurturance [and] nurturance—the love that sustains others—is a basic need, as basic as eating or sex."[10]

But complaining about the lack of nurturance does not convert the authority, it only strengthens the bond which rejection builds. To move beyond rejection or "negation" requires "recognition."

A Journey of Transformance

Sennett draws the language of negation and recognition from Hegel's *The Phenomenology of Spirit*, a long inner journey Hegel describes to suggest how the experience of authority might become less humiliating and more free in everyday life. The journey consists of four stages: stoicism, scepticism, unhappy consciousness, and rational consciousness. According to Sennett's analysis, modern disbelief and rejection of authority represents passage through the first two stages. But motion stops there. The third stage would involve "the unhappy consciousness [which] takes this sceptical knowledge about a social relationship inside; there is a lord and a bondsman in every human being."[11] In the fourth stage, that of rational consciousness, this interior knowledge again becomes social; what one feels in oneself one now recognizes in others.

Each stage is marked by crises of authority. But the changes occur *in the subjects*; they become different persons who deal with authority non-competitively, forcing the lord to modulate his own behavior. While Sennett admits that Hegel's view is enormously idealistic and spiritual, he does recognize that liberty is not happiness. Hence the expression "the unhappy consciousness" which experiences division within and faces the "final acknowledgement that a tyrant and a slave live in every human being . . . ." This recognition allows people to see themselves as participants in their own oppression and their own liberation. In Sennett's words, "The unhappy consciousness prompts people to believe in authority without believing in the omnipotence of a person in authority; neither the enemy nor salvation is outside the gates, both are desires within consciousness; to seek them as pure essences of other people is to lie to oneself."[12]

Sennett offers a poignant example of how disengagement allows one to reconceive his or her relationship to another. He recounts the story of Madeleine Gide, the wife of writer André Gide. She had dedicated much of her life and energies to nurturing his genius in spite of his sexual infidelities. In the wake of an affair he had with a seventeen-year-old boy whose education had been entrusted to Gide, Madeleine Gide finally rebelled. She began to re-read and burn one by one over two thousand letters her husband had written to her since his youth. Gide himself said, "All the best of me I had entrusted to those letters." For Madeleine Gide, burning the letters addressed to her, was a way to break the spell which bound her so totally to his life at the expense of her own. After this ritual act, Madeleine Gide pursued her own interests and never again read any of her husband's books. Sennett comments:

> The consequences of this act were not to destroy their marriage, or even its outer appearance of stability. Rather, the legitimacy of Gide's demands for comfort and support was broken in her mind. He was no longer The Artist to whom all things were allowed in the name of his genius.

Sennett uses Madeleine Gide's story as an example of how one can change the malignant forms of authority in one's personal life. But the third stage of the journey is not enough. One must put these personal lessons to use in the public realm. This constitutes the fourth stage of the journey. Just as the third stage requires soul-searching so the fourth stage demands time and energy in requiring authority to be "visible" and "legible." Sennett argues that

> No person in power can be trusted to serve as his own judge and jury. It is the subjects who have to decide what power means; the servants have to read the masters' actions as though trying to make sense of a difficult text. To make power legible in this way was the aim of all the intimate struggles described [above]. The act of reading is always a reflexive activity: purging, masking, empathizing, losing one's fear are acts the subjects perform on themselves in order better to see and judge the authorities in their lives.[14]

A Biblical Reflection

Sennett's analysis makes clear that any call to conversion from destructive forms of authority in Church life must be addressed to both those in authority and those under it. Both *belong to the same generation.* We are all "children of the age" and we share the troublesome upbringing of a time in which the major patterns of authority are paternalism and autonomy. Moreover, we are faced with the reality that much of the language surrounding authority within the Roman Catholic community fosters and supports both modes but especially paternalism: the "Holy Father," "holy mother church," calling priests "Father," veneration of the Holy (nuclear) Family, devotion to Mary as the Virgin-Mother who is always present, self-giving, conforming and ever silent as the model woman in the church (as was Madeleine Gide!).

If Sennett is right about paternalism being a major form of authority in the modern world, then the Catholic Church is one of its more obvious examples. As a Catholic biblical scholar, I find myself more and more astonished at the force with which biblical metaphors and images challenge particularly the use of 'father' as a metaphor for authority within our faith communities. Each of the gospels offers stunning examples of images and metaphors which undermine the patriarchal system of that time and the paternalistic bent of ecclesiastical authority in our own.

The Gospel of Mark in many ways is a long meditation on the abuse of power.[15] We read of a startling episode early in the ministry of Jesus. He had, we are told, performed a cure of someone in the synagogue, healed large crowds, and chosen the Twelve to "be with him."

> Then he went home; but the crowd came together again, so that they could not even eat. And when his family heard it, they went out to seize him, for they said, "He is out of his mind" (3:20-21).

Immediately after this ominous note, the narrative continues:

> And the scribes who came down from Jerusalem said, "He is possessed by Beelzebul, and by the prince of demons he casts out the demon" (3:22).

In other words, the author of Mark's gospel portrays Jesus' human family among the outsiders who oppose him and who attempt to put an *interpretation* upon Jesus' person and actions contrary to his own. We are therefore prepared for the outcome in the following episode:

> And his mother and his brothers came; and standing outside they sent to him and called him. And a crowd was sitting about him; and they said to him, "Your mother and your brothers are outside, asking for you." And he replied, "Who are my mother and my brothers?" And looking around on those who sat about him, he said, "Here are my mother and my

brothers! Whoever does the will of God is my brother, and sister, and mother" (3:31-35).

In the Markan gospel Jesus' family of origin is never rehabilitated. His mother is not among the women who stand as witnesses to his death on the cross nor among those who first learn from the angel at the empty tomb that He is risen. What dominates instead is an image of Jesus whose identity comes from relationship with God. Again, in Mark's gospel, the naming of Jesus as "son" of God comes at a few choice moments in the story, the two most prominent being when he is baptized ("You are my beloved Son; with you I am well pleased"), and when he dies on the cross and the Roman centurion says "Truly this was the Son of God" (15:39).

A third and related Markan text is especially important. It portrays Jesus, faced with his death in the Garden of Gethsemane, praying to God as *abba*, father. The idea that saying *abba* was the language of intimacy used by children, equivalent to saying 'Daddy,' is perhaps one of the most commonly repeated ideas of modern scholarship. But the eminent philologist, James Barr, has recently disputed the work of Joachim Jeremias in this regard, arguing that *abba* was actually normal usage of adults. Moreover, within the gospel tradition, as Barr points out, Jesus is recorded as having used the expression of *abba* only once.[16] That one occasion was the prayer of Jesus in the Garden of Gethsemane.

The scene is especially instructive for Mark's message. For it invites us to confront the connection between Jesus who is about to suffer a most painful death and his calling God "father." He is soon to be abandoned by his twelve disciples and scornfully rejected by those in authority as well as by the crowds. At this point, his calling God "father" gives him no power over others but rather places him at their mercy. For Jesus, the claiming of God as father came at a terrible cost. He put loyalty to God before loyalty to family, to patriarchal power, and he paid for it with his life.

Matthew offers another example of the careful use of father imagery within the gospel tradition. In this gospel calling God "father" occurs often—some 45 times as compared with only four uses in Mark and 17 in Luke. It is owing to Matthew that we begin the Lord's Prayer with "Our Father who art in Heaven." The Lukan version, which is considered more ancient, begins simply with "Father." But Matthew's use of the metaphor of God as Father is critical precisely because he does not suggest that human fatherhood is a reflection of or participation in Divine Fatherhood. To the contrary, Matthew's predilection for calling God father, especially "the heavenly father," carries a heavy injunction. In the scene in which Jesus, like a fiery prophet, dresses down the scribes and Pharisees for abuse of their power and privilege, we read this stern imperative to his own followers:

> "Call no one on earth your father; for you have one father who is in heaven." (23:9)

To this is added: "Neither be called masters, for you have one master, the Christ. He who is greatest among you [meaning, whoever has the most power or authority] shall be your servant; whoever exalts himself will be humbled, and whoever humbles himself will be exalted" (23:10-12). Had Christian tradition remained faithful to these words of Jesus in the gospel, there would be less need to re-image authority in the Church today.

In her excellent study reconstructing the history of the early church, Elisabeth Schussler Fiorenza says Jesus sets the patriarchal system on its head.[17] The patriarch, the ruling father, was dethroned. But she sees Paul then putting the hierarchical pyramid back onto its side and the pastoral letters as standing patriarchy up on its feet. Paul slips badly in precisely his use of the image of being a father to the communities he founded.[18] Thus, in spite of Jesus' challenge to patriarchy, Christian civilization kept within the patriarchal system by moving from patriarchy to patrimonialism to paternalism.

If we presented our present experience of authority within the Church to Jesus and he asked, "Whose image and inscription does this experience bear?" we might look in vain for a resemblance to Jesus. But if we begin to change in our personal lives the malignant forms of authority which we suffer, then, I suspect, the image and inscription upon our experience of authority will very quickly become the cross.

The Sign of the Cross

Within the Fourth Gospel, one major symbol of Jesus' life is descending and then ascending. This motif finds expression in such familiar texts as John 3:13-15:

> No one has ascended into heaven but he who descended from heaven, the Son of Man. And as Moses lifted up the serpent in the wilderness, so must the son of man be lifted up, that whoever believes in him may have eternal life.

and John 13:12:31-33:

> "Now is the judgment of this world, now shall the ruler of this world be cast out; and I, when I am lifted up from the earth, will draw all beings to myself." He said this to show by what death he was to die.

Robert Bly is a poet who lectures widely on gender issues. He has distinguished himself as a leader in developing men's support groups. Most especially he is involved in resurrecting ancient myths in order to recover a holistic, healthy male consciousness, suggesting that healthy male consciousness will only come as one moves through the stage of "unhappy consciousness."[19] Bly claims that the myths most men live out of today are dysfunctional because they have no descending mode. Failure is not allowed men, it is forbidden, and where it exists, it is denied.

It would not be too strong to say that authority in the modern world is held by men and it is failing: failing to give life, failing to nurture, failing to work with nature instead of against it. Paternalism is ultimately destructive, malignant, and ought to be feared. For men to acknowledge that reality will require a kind of death, a descent.

Women will also have their own dying to do, not the least of which will be owning up to the denial which has been part of their oppression. But each year I find more women speaking out, more women voicing the pain, admitting their wounds. Recently, one of my students, in a course on Theology of the Feminine, drew inspiration from the writings of the French philosopher Luce Irigaray, in particular, her reading of medieval women mystics. These brave women spoke of doubting, even when they knew and felt within their experiences God comforting and accepting them. Their doubt arose from male confessors who questioned: "How could God reveal himself in all his magnificence and waste his substance on so weak and vile a creature as woman?" But these women did not acquiesce to the male/patriarchal mode of behavior. They loved God all the more.

My student wrote:

> What a beautiful reclamation for women, and what a beautiful way to honor and remember these women who suffered so horribly. Irigaray states that women are the ones who accepted and were not afraid of Jesus' wounds; who cared for him and did not fear to look upon his body when crucified: a wonderful

cleansing of our own wounds, and a wonderful image for us to retain.[20]

A wound is a hole, a rupture, a break. This is where women's lives and the story of Jesus come together. For patriarchy and paternalism have created deep ruptures in women's lives. One thinks easily of the women in the gospels who encountered Jesus out of their pain. The hemorrhaging woman who suffered at the hands of many physicians spent all she had, and only grew worse (Mark 5:25-34). The Syrophoenician woman, an outsider both racially and sexually, asserts herself, asking Jesus to cure her ailing daughter (Mark 8:24-30). Most especially, one thinks of the women who at the end stood looking on and who watched where his own torn and pierced body was laid (Mark 15:40-41, 47).

There is a saying that whoever tells the stories rules the world. Richard Sennett makes the same claim when he refers to authority as the power to interpret. Robert Bly cautions that the current myth in the West suppresses half of the male experience. Patriarchy—the rule of the fathers—suppresses all of women's experience, except that which is relevant to the stories of men. There is a wonderful reflection of this in the genealogy at the beginning of the Gospel of Matthew. The genealogy gives us Joseph's rich heritage as a Jew descended from the generations of Israel. Mary enters the story as an unknown. She has no roots, no background to speak of, no history, no story of her own. Yet after 39 times of genealogical "begats," of a male begetting a male, we read:

> "of Joseph the husband of Mary, of whom Jesus was born, who is called the Christ." (1:16)

In one stroke the patriarchal genealogy is overturned and the story of Jesus begins. It is that story, with its wonderful reversals, which can still speak to us and give new shape to authority within the Church so that our experience within church will bear ever more strongly and clearly the image and inscription of Christ. It is that story which calls for a conversion of imagination and a process of mutual empowerment within the Church.

Notes

1. Mark 12:16; Matt. 22:20; Luke 20:24.

2. Genesis 1:27. Cf. Garrett Green (*Imagining God: Theology and the Religious Imagination* [San Francisco: Harper & Row, 1989] pp. 105-106) who uses the language of *eikon* to underscore the importance of imagination in Christian faith and life.

3. Richard Sennett, *Authority* (New York: Alfred A. Knopf, 1980). See also Letty M. Russell, "Authority in Mutual Ministry," *Quarterly Review* (Spring, 1986) pp. 10-23; *Household of Freedom: Authority in Feminist Theology* (Philadelphia: Westminster Press, 1987).

4. *Authority*, p. 28.

5. To quote Sennett: "In a paternalistic society, males continue to dominate. The domination is based on their roles as fathers: protectors, stern judges, the strong. But this basis is symbolic rather than material as in patrimonial order. In a paternalistic society no father can guarantee to his children a known place in the world; he can only act protectively" (p. 54).

6. *Authority*, p. 51.

7. *Authority*, p. 57. For an even more devastating critique of the social contract theory as establishing modern patriarchy, see Carole Pateman, *The Sexual Contract* (Stanford University Press: Stanford, CA, 1988).

8. *Authority*, p. 68.

9. *Authority*, p. 82.

10. *Authority*, p. 120.

11. *Authority*, p. 128.

12. *Authority*, pp. 31-32.

13. *Authority*, p. 140. One might be tempted to see Madeleine Gide as a victim whose suffering brought her knowledge and insight. But Sennett quarrels with those who would idealize suffering. For just as some use the suffering of the unfortunate in their own drives for power, Sennett argues, "one commits something of the same sin by taking the oppressed as 'models,' as people who are 'really' dealing with life, people more solid and substantial then oneself." But if people rather "focus on how they react to being hurt as the real problem, then at least they will cease to value their injuries; they will not conspire at their own suffering" (pp. 150-153).

14. *Authority*, p. 168.

15. See Donald Senior, " 'With Swords and Clubs . . .' The Setting of Mark's Community and His Critique of Abusive Power," *Biblical Theology Bulletin* 17 (1987) pp. 10-20.

16. James Barr, "Abba Isn't 'Daddy' " *Journal of Theological Studies* 39 (1988), pp. 28-47. A more popular version of the article appears in " 'Abba, Father,' and the Familiarity of Jesus' Speech," *Theology* 91 (1988), pp. 173-179.

17. Elizabeth Schussler Fiorenza, *In Memory of Her* (Crossroad: New York, 1983).

18. E.g., 1 Corinthians 5:14-15: "I am writing you this not to shame you, but to admonish you as my beloved children. Even if you should have countless guides to Christ, yet you do not have many fathers, for I became your father in Christ Jesus through the gospel." Notice that Jesus himself never uses father images to refer to himself.

19. See, e.g., *A Gathering of Men* with Bill Moyers and Robert Bly, a production of Public Affairs Television, Inc.: New York, 1990.

20. Quoted from Christine Chapin's study of "La Mysterique" in Luce Irigaray's book *Speculum*.

8

Issues Orbiting Church Authority

Michael B. Raschko
The Archdiocese of Seattle, and
The Institute for Theological Studies
Seattle University

Authority does not function in a vacuum. Its use is shaped by the way we understand both the physical and social worlds, by psychological drives and needs, by our personal and social histories, and by our relationships and commitments. Much more is going on in relationships based on authority than an organizational chart or a list of goals and objectives reveals.

This disparity holds true as well for authority in the Church. However spiritual its foundation, however pious its apologetics might be, authority in the Church is shaped by these same forces. To ignore this reality and to continue to use power in the name of service is dangerous, for we then become blind to the realities that shape our relationships within the Church.

There are four areas I would like to address which shape how authority functions in the Church but are not usually discussed when authority is the issue on the table. I will not be able to do too much more than raise questions around the issues and perhaps indicate some directions for further reflection and research.

Jus Divinum

The first area for exploration is that of *jus divinum*. The term is usually applied to those offices, structures and actions of the Church which have been divinely mandated and instituted and so are not subject to alteration or removal by human agency. Problems begin to arise when we try to name what in the life of the Church is a matter of *jus divinum* and what is a matter of *jus humanum*, that is, constituted by human freedom and creativity. For example, it is clear in the Roman Catholic tradition that the office of the bishops as successors of the apostles is *de jure divino*. We cannot and dare not do away with it. It is also fully clear that the system for cataloguing books in the Vatican library is not divinely mandated. It is a human creation and can be changed at any time. The territory between these two clear extremes can get cloudy quickly.

Karl Rahner asked toward the end of his life whether the office of bishop, that divinely mandated function of carrying on the leadership of the community and preserving the apostolic tradition, might not be carried out by a committee or a college.[1] The role and function of the episcopal office is divinely ordered and essential to the life of the Church, but is how we organize to carry out that function and office open to change? Is authority in the Church tied to individual persons, or is it tied to functions and roles? Karl Rahner was simply asking a question, exploring theological possibilities. His thought experiment was not aimed at a discussion of how the office of bishop ought to be organized, but at the issue of the interplay of the divine and the human in the structure and functioning of the Church.

Similar questions can be asked about the sacraments. There is no doubt in the mind of most Christians that the eucharist is a matter of *jus divinum*. We have a clear New Testament mandate from Jesus to "do this in memory of me." But how it has been done through the centuries has a wonderfully rich history of diversity and development. Where does the divine institution end and the product of human freedom begin?

The topic of the sacraments raises further questions. The Council of Trent stated that there are seven sacraments divinely instituted by Christ. There is no *jus humanum* there. But for over a millennium it had not been settled either how many sacraments there were, nor which were to be included in the list. Obviously there is historical development in the thought on both questions, but can something that is divinely instituted develop and therefore change historically? If it does develop, doesn't human agency play a role?

If we do not accept some type of historical development, we could find ourselves in what Avery Dulles calls the Neo-Lutheran view of Edmund Schlink.[2] This position holds that there are four essential, divinely constituted elements in the Church: a) proclaiming God's saving deed, b) baptism, c) eucharist, d) and the power to bind and loose. There is a need for an orderly way of carrying out these divinely constituted elements of the Church, but the organization and functions of carrying them out is a matter of human creativity. Hans Küng is close to this position when he holds that Church office can legitimately develop according to human authority and all forms of church government are reformable.

At the other end of the theological spectrum we find the non-historical Roman Catholic manualist view that the Lord gave the Church everything it would need for the duration of its existence. Everything is there in the apostolic deposit of faith if you just know how to ferret it out. These claims reach beyond even those of Trent which saw the need for the authority to change the sacramental rituals of the Church.

Within a framework of historical consciousness, the manualist tradition is in trouble. All within the apostolic deposit has not come from Jesus. Rahner caught this insight and saw the need for recognition of the role the Holy Spirit in ecclesiological developments.[3] Thus historical developments could be *de jure divino* and therefore irreversible. But others question whether *de jure divino* developments might not be culturally bound and therefore open to further developments and reversibility.

The issues here are complicated. They involve permanence and mutability, history and essentiality, freedom and destiny, the divine and the human. Dulles is helpful in his sorting out of four concentric spheres of ecclesiastical structures to which *jus divinum* applies in varying degrees.[4] In the innermost sphere are situated those elements of Church life which can be traced to Jesus and are essential to the Church. Included would be a ministries of proclamation, pastoral care, leadership, baptism and eucharist, and a community centered on forgiveness. Clear claims can be made for the fact that these elements belong to the Church *de jure divino*. Without them we would not be Church.

In the second sphere are those elements which developed in the post apostolic age but can be traced to a biblical basis. These too would be irreversible *de jure divino* elements and would include the creeds, the sacraments, and ministerial structures such as the episcopacy. How they are shaped and function is, however, still a matter open to human agency.

The third sphere includes those elements that are *de jure divino* because they are willed by Christ and inspired by the Holy Spirit but are clearly responses to the needs of a particular period. They are, therefore, not only quite open to change but may even cease to be part of the Church's life.

Finally, the fourth sphere contains those elements which are "merely" human products, neither willed by God nor contrary to the divine will.

All that is fairly clear until the question is raised about criteria to distinguish which elements of the Church belong in which sphere. Then the distinctions are no longer as clear, and battles begin to loom. Does the question of the ordination of women belong in the first, second, third or fourth sphere? The stakes are high for authority in the Church, for how you think through the issue of *jus divinum* determines what areas of Church life are open to change through Church authority, how that authority can be structured, and who might have access to that authority.

Though the whole topic is crucially important, I think it could be misconceived. What is central to the discussion is how the divine and the human interact. It is a theme which runs through ecclesiology but has deeper roots in the theology of grace and in Christology. It really is a question of incarnation, so perhaps some of our central clues need to come from Christology.

In Christology, the relationship of the divine and the human receives its classic expression from the Council of Chalcedon, which holds that the divine and human natures come together in the person of Jesus without confusion or change, without division or separation. The Church Fathers said at that Council that full divinity and full humanity are both operative in Jesus without either being fundamentally changed. However, they expressed this using the intellectual tools at hand—fifth century Greek notions of nature, which have led us into some intellectual traps since then. One of them is the eagle/rabbit notion of the divine and the human in Jesus and in the life of the Church. We have two different kinds of entities which are put together in one being, like a rabbit and an eagle. When it hops, it's the rabbit nature at work; when it flies, we have the eagle nature before us. When Jesus heals a blind man, it's the divine nature at work; when he is moved deeply and cries at the tomb of Lazarus, obviously we are dealing with the passible human nature. The question I would like to put forward is this: what if Jesus crying at the tomb of Lazarus is a clearer indication of the divinity than the supernatural power to heal? What if the power to heal is rooted in something far more basic to divinity and humanity, namely, compassion?

Far too often we assume theologically that divinity is another thing or kind of being alongside eagles, rabbits and human beings. It is not. It is utterly beyond any finite structure and to use a term like divine nature is to use analogical language which has its negative as well as its positive elements.

Rather than simply distinguishing some elements as proper to the divine nature and others to the human, would we not be better off asking what human elements are open to bearing and expressing the divine both in Christology and ecclesiology? Thus the compassion of Jesus, a human element, would be an area of his life in which divinity is most clearly expressed and which is the *sine qua non* needed for divine power to be incarnate and heal. Perhaps divine power and divine authority can only be incarnate in history in human forms of life, organization, and order. There would still be irreversible elements in the life of the Church, but their status would not rest in the fact that they are the furthest from being products of human freedom, development and creativity, but rather because they are precisely the most truly human. They go to the core of what it means to be human and so are capable of imaging the divine. The sacramental system of the Catholic Church is a matter of *jus divinum*, but it builds on the basis of such human realities as married love, forgiveness, communal meals, sickness and death. Authority in the Church is a matter of *jus divinum*, but any good reading of history will reveal how its structure and practice are rooted in cultural practices.

The implications of such a view of the interaction of the divine and the human could be profound for the theme of authority in the Church, in how it is structured, how it ought to operate, and what is amenable to change.

The Analogical Circle

The second constellation of issues centers on what, for lack of a better term, can be called the analogical circle. A few images will serve to illustrate the main point. On the Arch of Constantine in Rome is a small frieze which depicts the emperor seated on his throne in the center surrounded by his officials. The throne is elevated, placing the emperor above those who are pictured with him. He is seated, immovable, at the center and yet is the source of the action which surrounds him. From him flows the bounty of the empire.

A second image comes from the 5th century apse mosaic in the Roman Church of St. Pudenziana. The similarities are striking. Christ in triumph is seated among his officials (bishops and saints). He too is raised slightly above the others to show his superiority and authority. He too holds his hand in a gesture of blessing, through which the bounty of his rule is bestowed upon his followers.

The imperial program here is clear. The authority of the emperor and the authority of Christ reflect and support one another. To challenge one would be to challenge the other. One comes to understand divine authority by understanding the authority of the emperor, or vice versa. The source of the emperor's authority lies in his mandate from heaven.

This ideological framework can be found throughout much of the art of the later empire, but it is not isolated to that world. The same theme can be found in a depiction of the Germanic emperor, Otto III, in a book of the Gospels which bears his name. It dates from about the year 1000. And finally, it can be seen again in many sculptures of Christ seated in triumph in the portals of medieval cathedrals.

The practice is not limited to the pictorial arts. It can be found in the language we use to speak of God, in our ways of governing, and in other church practices. Any knight from the world of feudalism would immediately recognize what is happening in the 20th century when a candidate for ordination places his hands in those of the bishop and promises obedience and respect. Such a rite is a borrowed practice of social organization which is used by the Church in its governing structures and is read into our relationship with God.

The analogical circle in these various examples has three movements. First, we use images drawn from human experience to picture or speak of God, or in this case of Christ in triumph. As theologian after theologian in the Christian tradition has reminded us, we have no other route to conceptualize the divine except through symbols and analogies. Therefore, when we want to talk about divine authority, divine triumph, divine bounty, we must appeal to our human experiences of these realities. The second movement is one of legitimation. Having borrowed certain social patterns and ways of ordering human experience to talk about the divine, we then claim that those social patterns and ways of ordering life are rooted in the divine and are legitimate because they have a foundation not in human wisdom but in the divine will. The third movement is simply one of imitation. Having legitimated social patterns by rooting them in the divine, we then seek to imitate the divine in the way we live. We must because it is the God-given order of reality.

The first thing that must be said about this analogical circle is that it is necessary. Each of its movements is important. We have no way to speak of the divine except through analogy. We have a deep need to root the order we find in creation and in human society in something ultimate. And we seek to imitate that which we value so much that we believe it is rooted in the divine.

Given that necessity, however, there are some questions that must be raised that have a profound impact on the theme of authority in the Church. First, do we recognize the analogical circle for what it is so that there is room for prophetic critique? The movement we most often forget is the first, the fact that our ways of imaging God emerge from human experience. One of the tasks of the prophet is to remind us that our language for God is always inadequate, that God remains a mystery full of surprises for his people. Curiously, once we think we have God nailed down, we then have a platform for nailing one another! To recognize the circle is to make room for prophetic critique and for the recognition of a variety of analogies to speak of the divine and a plurality of ways to live out our relationship with God.

Secondly, recognizing the circle not only reminds us that our images for God always come up short, and, therefore we dare not divinize our authority structures to too great a degree. Furthermore, it also reminds us that those images came from human experience in the first place. That is well and good, but the question can be quickly raised, whose experience counts. A study of the history of authority in the Church shows how much it bears the marks of the various epochs in which it lived. Some of the trappings and ideology of Roman and Byzantine imperialism are still with us as well as vestiges of medieval feudalism and early modern theories of the divine rights of kings. We borrow from culture. Having done so in the past, can we not do so again in the future, or are there certain epochs in our history which are more revelatory of the divine than others? Has not the recent history of the West uncovered such themes as the rights and dignity of the individual, and the need for participative forms of decision-making? The church will never be a voting democracy, but perhaps it is time we quit using that as an excuse not to explore some of the nuances of authority and power that have been learned since the emergence of democracy in the west in the Eighteenth Century. We might not only learn something new about how authority might function in the Church, but also about divine.

Finally, there are some questions to be asked about the spiritual price that imperial, monarchical images and uses of authority exact. These images tend to set all levels of authority from the divine on down above, over and often against those over whom they have authority. They lead to such operative images as Lord and Servant, creator and object created, ruler and ruled, the subject and the object of the narrowly defined rational subject, spirit/mind over matter, humanity subjugating the rest of creation. These images for God, for human relationships and for our place in creation have brought about an emphasis on distance between things rather than on unity and participation, an emphasis on strangeness and otherness which has separated us from God, one another and creation. They emphasize how the will of one is imposed on another rather than how one can empower another. They interpret our relationship with God and our salvation in juristic rather than organic terms.

Sexuality

My third constellation of issues centers around the theme of sexuality. It may be a bit of a mystery what sexuality has to do with authority in the Church, so I would take my first clue from the long list of sexual issues with which Church authority seems to be absorbed: birth control, abortion, celibacy, the ordination of women, altar girls, whether women can lector or be eucharistic ministers, homosexuality, homosexuality among priests, pedophilia, genetic technology. Each issue deeply touches authority in the Church either in the Church's eagerness to deal with the issue and proclaim moral norms or church laws, or in the Church's total avoidance of such painful realities as pedophilia and homosexuality among priests and other ecclesial leaders.

The second clue to the relationship of sexuality and authority lies in the great weight these issues receive both from those in authority and from those over whom that authority is exercised. How many people are upset by John XXIII's *Pacem in Terris* or Paul VI's *Populorum Progressio*; but they all know the teaching of Paul VI in *Humani Vitae*. We know that a bishop or a theologian who disagrees with the birth control encyclical can find himself in deep trouble with Vatican authorities, but has any disciplinary action ever been taken against bishops who are allied with oppressive governments in Central and South America? Except for the American bishops' statement on the economy, when has church authority ever shaken anyone by its pronouncements on business ethics, an area of life that can be every bit as destructive of men and women as sexual ethics? The ties between sexuality and church authority run much deeper, at least on an unconscious level, than those between church authority and social justice.

A third clue lies in the denial of sexuality that takes place in so many levels of the Church. Sexuality was rarely discussed openly in my formation as a priest. I'm not sure that it is today, but the fact that the Vatican wants to move in the direction of not allowing women to act as spiritual directors of seminarians and not allowing women to be in classes with seminarians may give us a hint at how much seminary formation will deal with issues of sexuality. Other reasons may be given for these moves, but we must wonder what really is at play beneath the surface. How many men have reached positions of power within the Church without ever addressing their sexuality, without ever having had a wholesome relationship with a woman, and without really knowing how to interact with women? So, while we are in some ways obsessed with sexual issues in the Church, we are also caught in a pattern of avoidance and denial.

A pattern of obsession and avoidance is especially dangerous in the area of sexuality because sexuality is such a powerful psychological force. One does not have to be Freudian to recognize its power. But not to admit its power and to let it float through our lives unacknowledged and yet playing a powerful if unnamed role is dangerous, because our decisions and our relationships are being shaped by a force we refuse to recognize.

It would take a psychologist, or perhaps a team of them from various schools of thought, to explain adequately why sexuality has this kind of power in our lives, but I would like to point to two reasons why its power must be recognized in any discussion of authority in the Church. In the first place, our sexuality is one of the areas where human beings are most vulnerable. It is a place where we can be radically open to sharing ourselves with another human being, and where we can be the most protective and closed. It is a reality we often fear because sexuality is one of the profound ways we have of coming face to face with the mystery we are to ourselves, and it is a place where we can be easily manipulated. Given all this, the Church rightly speaks out on issues involving sexuality, but the Church's own thought on sexuality and relationships needs to mature and those in authority must be in the process of coming to terms with their own sexuality if it is not to remain a hidden force and a means of manipulation and control.

Secondly, the power of sexuality must be dealt with by the Church because of its holiness. Sexuality is holy because it is one of the routes to the deepest mysteries of our own being and a sacred place where we come to know our God. Sexuality is sacramental. St. John speaks of the fact that God is love, and anyone who abides in love abides in God and God in them. Our God is not a person who loves and is loved, but a relationship. That is one of the profound reasons why we Christians believe in a Trinitarian God. A divine person sitting alone through all eternity makes no sense to Christianity. A God who is love must be involved with another. Thus we believe God is triune, the Father, Son and Spirit. That which defines their interaction, their common nature, is love.

So where in life do we experience a God who is love? We need to look to our relationships and our sexuality. They are a highly privileged place where we come to know our God. Leadership, authority in the Church ought to be speaking to this area of our lives, to open up its sacramentality, not wall off an area of fear and vulnerability.

Sexuality and power are deeply connected with one another because sexuality is such a powerful psychological force and because it is holy. To deal well with authority in the Church we must come to terms with both of these aspects of its mystery.

Hermeneutics

The fourth area of concern I would like to address centers on the theme of hermeneutics. In short, what I would like to propose is that authority in the Roman Catholic Church must be hermeneutically conscious and hermeneutically structured. I would push that even further and say that those in authority cannot govern effectively today without consciously operating under the rubric of some hermeneutic.

The reasons such awareness is needed are twofold. In the first place, as Karl Rahner has stated, we are moving into the third great epoch in the history of Roman Catholicism.[5] The first was the short period of Judaic Christianity, when Christianity was attached to the Jewish synagogue. The second epoch followed quickly after the destruction of Jerusalem in 70 A.D. and lasted until about 1960. In it Roman Catholicism was embedded in Western European civilization. With Vatican II we have begun to move into the third period in which Roman Catholicism is no longer a Western European phenomenon, but a multi-cultural, pluricentered historical reality.

But the cultural diversity is not new. It is also present in the tradition of the West as it moved through its many varied epochs. The cultural matrix of late antiquity was different from that of the high middle ages, which in turn was different from the modern period with its roots in the Enlightenment. Who knows what the post-modern period which is in the midst of its birth pangs will look like? The Church has flourished in each epoch expressing its truths, working out its organizational structures, and living its faith through the cultural forms each epoch made available to it.

Both types of cultural diversity, historical and geographical call for an authority which is hermeneutically informed. If those in leadership in the Church are going to enable the Church to live its faith in today's world, they must enable a conversation between the cultural and ecclesial worlds of the past and those of today. The conversation should respect those different worlds and yet allow for a fusion of horizons in which new possibilities of being and expressing Christianity emerge. Note that it is a fusion of horizons. What was incarnate in past cultural forms finds new possibilities of expression, structure and life; and the present cultural epoch finds new modes or possibilities of being opened to it by what it is confronted with in the strange world of earlier Christian epochs. Authority must enable that conversation. For it not to do so, for it simply to preserve the past as if it were ahistorical and eternal, is both naïve and tragic: naïve in its lack of historical consciousness, and tragic in its closing off new possibilities for the expression and development of the Christian faith.

The same kind of hermeneutical conversation must take place among the cultures in which Roman Catholicism finds itself, especially between the central authority of Roman Catholicism and its many cultural centers. The same recognition of the other person and his or her world as other, the same fusion of horizons, and the same opening of possible modes of being must happen as the Vatican deals with the many local churches in their various cultures. This mutuality should involve a hermeneutics of suspicion, that is, a prophetic call which challenges both the Vatican and the local church to let go of those elements of its life which destroy or distort the gospel. It will also involve a hermeneutics of retrieval, in which the heart of the gospel finds new modes of expression.

A failure to deal with the multicultural reality of Roman Catholicism with a hermeneutically conscious approach is tragic because it spells the loss of new cultural opportunities for the life of Christianity, and it is immoral because it remains caught in a pattern, whether consciously or not, of cultural imperialism.

Conclusion

Jus divinum and the relationship of the human and the divine, the analogical circle, sexuality, and hermeneutics: that is quite a diverse list of subjects for a talk on authority in the Church. I would finish by making two key points. First, authority in the Church will not be well addressed theoretically or well handled practically until issues like these which orbit it are dealt with. And secondly, there is a common theme to the four issues dealt with in this paper. That common theme can be put in the form of a mandate: to deal well with authority in the Church theoretically and practically we must come to terms with our humanity.

Notes

1. Karl Rahner, "Aspects of the Episcopal Office," *Theological Investigations, Vol. 14, Ecclesiology, Questions in the Church, The Church in the World,* New York: Seabury Press, 1976, p. 191.

2. Avery Dulles, *A Church to Believe in, Discipleship and the Dynamics of Freedom,* New York: Crossroad, 1982, pp. 87-88, 95-96.

3. Karl Rahner, *Op. cit.,* p. 189.

4. Avery Dulles, *Op. cit.,* pp. 95-100.

5. Karl Rahner, "Towards a Fundamental Theological Interpretation of Vatican II," 4 *Theological Studies,* Vol. 40, pp. 716 ff.

Contributors to this Volume

Dr. Karen Barta is Associate Professor in Biblical Studies, Department of Theology and Religious Studies at Seattle University. Dr. Barta, a well-known lecturer, has her Ph.D. from Marquette University. She is the author of *The Gospel of Mark,* and is an active member in the biblical guild.

Dr. Gary Chamberlain is Professor of Christian Ethics at Seattle University. A graduate of the Graduate Theological Union of Berkeley, California, he is chair of the Department of Theology and Religious Studies and the former Director of SUMORE, a graduate program in ministry and religious education. His most recent writings include *Fostering Faith* from Paulist Press.

Fr. Peter Chirico, S.S., is Professor of Systematic Theology at the Institute for Theological Studies, Seattle University. From 1978-1986, he served as Theologian-in-Residence for the Archdiocese of Seattle. He is the author of *Infallibility: The Crossroads of Doctrine.*

Fr. Patrick Howell, S.J., is Associate Professor in the Institute for Theological Studies, Seattle University, where he serves as co-director of the Master of Divinity and Master of Theological Studies programs. He completed his Doctor of Ministry at the Catholic University of America and is the author of *Reducing the Storm to a Whisper.*

Fr. Richard McBrien is the Crowly-O'Brien-Walter Professor of Theology at the University of Notre Dame and chair of its Department of Theology. He is a priest of the archdiocese of Hartford, Connecticut, with a doctorate in theology from the Gregorian University in Rome. He is the author of 14 books, most recently *Ministry: A Theological, Pastoral Handbook.*

Sr. Ann Patrick, S.N.J.M., is Associate Professor and Chair of the Religion Department, Carleton College. She served as President of the Catholic Theological Society of America, 1989-1990. Her most recent publication is "Character and Community: Curran and a Church Coming of Age," in *Vatican Authority and American Catholic Dissent,* ed. by William W. May.

Fr. Michael Raschko is a priest of the Seattle Archdiocese, Theological Resource for the Archdiocese, and a member of the faculty of the Institute for Theological Studies, Seattle University. Fr. Raschko has a doctorate from the University of Chicago.

Fr. Michael Scanlon, O.S.A., is Professor of Systematic Theology at Washington Theological Union. He was President of the Catholic Theological Society of America, 1987-1988, and Co-Founder and Second President of the Washington Theological Consortium. Recent articles include: "Christian Anthropology," and "Hope" in *Theological Dictionary,* Michael Glazier.

Sr. Mary Ellen Sheehan, B.V.M., is an Associate Professor in Theology at the University of St. Michael's College, and a member of the Toronto School of Theology. A graduate of the Catholic University of Louvain, Belgium, with a STD degree, she is currently specializing in the correlation of theory and praxis as that relationship expresses itself in church issues.

Fr. David Tracy, is Professor at The Divinity School, University of Chicago. He is past President of the Catholic Theological Society of America and serves on the boards of *Concilium, Journal of Religion,* and *Religious Studies Review.* His recent works include *Religion in the Public Realm* and *Plurality and Ambiguity: Hermeneutics, Religion and Hope.*

Vatican Investigation: Chronology of Events

November 1983 Vatican sends Archbishop James Hickey of Washington, D.C., on an official, six-day visit to Seattle to investigate criticisms of Archbishop Raymond G. Hunthausen's ministry.

September 1985 Archbishop Hunthausen receives a letter from Cardinal Joseph Ratzinger, Prefect of the Congregation for the Doctrine of the Faith, citing Vatican concerns about his ministry regarding the marriage tribunal, intercommunion, homosexual men and women, use of general absolution, sequence of first confession and first Communion, the role of women and other matters.

November 1985 Archbishop Hunthausen releases letter from papal pronuncio Archbishop Pio Laghi affirming the end of the two-year investigation.

December 1985 Archbishop Laghi announces that the Vatican has appointed Father Donald Wuerl, a priest of the Diocese of Pittsburgh, as auxiliary bishop to Archbishop Hunthausen.

March 1986 Bishop Wuerl states that he has special faculties given to him by the Vatican; Archbishop Hunthausen seeks clarification from Rome.

September 1986 Archbishop Hunthausen announces that the Vatican has given final authority to Bishop Wuerl in five key areas of ministry. Thousands of church members in Western Washington sign a petition asking that Archbishop Hunthausen's full faculties be restored.

January 1987 Vatican appoints Apostolic Commission—Cardinal Joseph Bernardin of Chicago, Cardinal John O'Connor of New York and Archbishop John Quinn of San Francisco—to assess the Seattle situation.

May 1987 Acting on the commission's recommendations, the Vatican restores Archbishop Hunthausen's full authority, transfers Bishop Wuerl to Pittsburgh, and appoints Bishop Thomas J. Murphy of Great Falls-Billings, Montana, as coadjutor archbishop of Seattle with right of succession.

October 1988 Last of five meetings held between commission and Archbishops Hunthausen and Murphy, in which they identified issues of Vatican concern, formalized a response and developed means to implement the response.

December 1988 Archbishops Hunthausen and Murphy visit Pope John Paul II in Rome and express optimism that the Vatican review would soon be closed.

April 1989 Archbishop Laghi announces an end to the Apostolic Commission's review of the Seattle Archdiocese.

(Prepared by *The Seattle Progress*, April 13, 1989, p. 10.)